Everything is peaceful. You're relaxed in your favorite chair, listening to the newest record when the phone rings.

"Hi, I need your help." It's the youth director at church. Since you're feeling good you reply, "Sure, what's up?"

"We need a camp counselor. It's just a week and you'll only have about eight or so kids. Will you do it?" You say yes and hang up. But all of a sudden the magnitude of the job hits you. *Help, I'm a Camp Counselor!*

This book will answer whatever questions you may have.

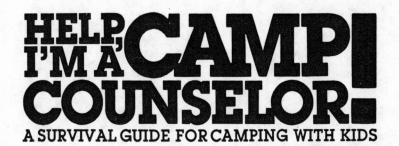

HELP, I'M A CAMP COUNSELOR!

A SURVIVAL GUIDE FOR CAMPING WITH KIDS

H. NORMAN WRIGHT
& MICHAEL J. ANTHONY

HELP, I'M A CAMP COUNSELOR!

A SURVIVAL GUIDE FOR CAMPING WITH KIDS

Regal Books

A Division of GL Publications
Ventura, California, U.S.A.

Rights for publishing this book in other languages are contracted by Gospel Litera-
ture International (GLINT) foundation. GLINT also provides technical help for
the adaptation, translation, and publishing of Bible study resources and books in
scores of languages worldwide. For further information, contact GLINT, Post
Office Box 6688, Ventura, California 93006, U.S.A. or the publisher.

Published by Regal Books
A Division of GL Publications
Ventura, California 93006
Printed in U.S.A.

Library of Congress Cataloging in Publication Data

Wright, H. Norman
    Help, I'm a camp counselor!

    Bibliography: p.
    Includes index.
    1. Camps—Management. 2. Camp counselors.
3. Church camps—Management. I. Anthony, Michael J.
II. Title.
GV198.M35W74   1986   796.54′22′068   85-28120
ISBN 0-8307-1108-2

Editor's note: For the sake of easier reading, the use of *he, him* and *his* in this publication refers for the most part to both male and female in the generic sense.

To the memory of Dr. Bill V. Bynum, for his commitment to Christian camping and dedicated years of service in the field of Christian education.

Contents

1
The Ministry of Christian Camping

The Biblical Significance of Camping

Throughout the history of mankind, God has chosen to communicate with man through the use of outdoor settings. The Garden of Eden, the wandering of His people in the wilderness, giving the law from Mount Sinai, Jesus teaching on mountains, by the lakeshore and on the plains, even His death on Mount Calvary—all were His attempt to minister to the needs of people through the use of a natural setting.

This desire of God to communicate with man has continued up to the present time. Today in North America it is estimated that there are over 2,000 Christian camps in operation. Since its beginning in North America in 1880, Christian camping has been reaching out to the needs of man with the message that God loves him and desires a relationship with him.

Never before in the history of our country has camping reached such a prominent place in the hearts and minds of individuals. Yet this is just the beginning; the Golden Age of camping has just begun. Camping has been on the uprise since the turn of the century. It has been used for personal and individual growth, and, in the case of the Jugend camps used by Hitler to train young Germans, camping has also served national purposes. But there is a uniqueness to the *Christian* camping program that sets it apart from others: it seeks to develop the total person, not only in relationship to himself and others, but also to God. Thus his life has a purpose and there is the possibility of a complete change taking place in the individual.

Benefits for the Camper

Campers, both young and old, can become aware of the presence of God as they establish a new sensitivity toward the creation of God. They are able to see and appreciate the beauty of nature which God has made and established. The change of pace in their daily life and environment makes them more perceptive and observant. The well-established plan and order of God in His creation is evident as the campers see the marvels of nature. Through this awareness and the program of the camp, individuals are led to see God's perfect plan in the person of Jesus Christ.

Because Christ is central in the camping program, campers of all ages may either come to meet Him face-to-face for the first time, or may renew, in a living and vital way, their relationship with God. It is estimated that one-fourth of all Christians make their decision at a Christian camp. One denomination in America discovered that one-third of their missionaries made their decision to go to the mission field while at a camp. Although it is true that Christians go to camp to have fun and good times, they also go to camp looking for solutions to many of their problems. They go looking for challenge and enrichment that will enable them to be leaders in the Christian faith and their community. They go looking for guidance so that they are able to maintain an unbroken relationship with Jesus Christ when they leave camp and return home. They want to know how to live and survive as Christians! They face and learn to handle these questions and others, by learning during actual-life situations at camp rather than in the formal teaching situation. Camp, in one sense, is a training ground for Christian principles; a place where relationships are learned, tested and tried.

Learning takes place each moment the camper is awake and the educators are not just the speakers but each staff member, the environment, and the other campers.

Benefits for the Church

The average Christian spends approximately three to four hours in Bible related activities each week at church. In a week at camp that same Christian may spend over six times as many hours in Bible teaching and worship activities. It is not surprising that evidence over the years has indicated that camp is one of the most powerful and effective tools in the development of the Christian person. Camping offers an opportunity for achieving the Christian education objectives of the local church program.

Today, as never before in the history of Christian camping, there are opportunities for extensive appeal. The diversity of programs that many camps offer help reach an even broader spectrum of Christian needs. There are camps which specialize in programs to teach Sunday School teachers, train lay leaders, evangelize youth, communicate the needs of missions and many other important areas of church education. The broad scope of camps today has helped to make Christian camping a vibrant and dynamic ministry in America.

The Goals of Christian Camping

The goals of Christian camping vary from camp to camp and from church to church. The Philosophy Committee of the National Sunday School Association Camp Commissions has provided evangelical Christians with a list of objectives for camps.

The Christian camp should provide opportunities:

1. to deal with campers as individuals, counseling them personally in the areas of their spiritual need (note Jesus' example in John 3;5);

2. to encourage definite spiritual decision at the level of the camper's readiness (as in Jesus' example in the same chapters in John);

3. to help establish good habits of Christian living—prayer, Bible reading and study, personal devotions and witnessing (2 Tim. 3:14-17; Acts 1:8; 2:42);

4. to have practical experience in leadership, service, witnessing and application of spiritual truths to daily living (2 Tim. 2:2; John 13:1-17; Luke 22:24-28; Mark 6:7).

In addition, the Christian camp seeks other outcomes related to the total development of the camper, such as:

1. the establishment of sound health habits—cleanliness, adequate rest, proper diet, wholesome exercise and good attitudes toward the body as God's temple (1 Cor. 6:19,20);

2. the profitable and wise use of leisure, independent of artificial machine-made amusements (Eph. 5:15,16);

3. learning outdoor skills as a means of developing character and as training for possible future missionary work (1 Cor. 9:19-27; 10:31);

4. development of the ability to get along with others unselfishly (1 Cor. 13; Rom. 12:9-21);

5. learning effective leadership skills (Exod. 35:30-35);

6. learning responsibility for one's own decisions (Gal. 6:4-9).[1]

Questions for Further Discussion

1. Other than those presented in chapter 1, can you identify any camping experiences from the Old Testament or New Testament? What is the significance of those experiences?
2. If you attended camp as a youth, can you remember any special experiences that were helpful and beneficial to you? What made your experiences so special?

3. Why do you think so many Christians made their decision to follow Christ in the context of a Christian camp?
4. Why do you think so many missionaries chose to go to the mission field while they were attending a Christian camp?
5. Reread the goals of Christian camping. Of those listed, which goals are most significant to you? Why?

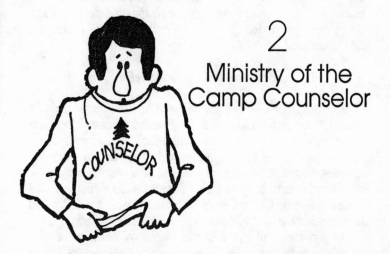

2
Ministry of the Camp Counselor

Each year millions of children, youth and adults attend camp. The experiences of this time have lasting effects and influence their development and total perspective on life. Indeed there are many factors which influence the camper, factors such as the location of the camp, the atmosphere of the physical surroundings, the quality of the food, and the thrust and message of the speakers. Yet none of these factors will have more of an influence upon the camper than *you*, the counselor.

Counseling at camp will present many opportunities as well as certain requirements. Why should you consider camp counseling? What are the benefits, the challenges, the requirements and the cost? What will you have to do and what will you have to learn? Questions like these will flicker through your mind when you are confronted with the invitation and challenge of a counseling experience. What will the camp experience mean and do for you? One of the benefits of being at camp for a weekend or summer is the enjoyment of the beautiful surroundings that God has created. There will be memories of the clear sky during the day and the vast expanse of sparkling stars in the evening. Swimming in the pool or lake, canoeing, hiking up the trail or exploring new regions, amusing experiences with other counselors and campers, challenge and growth during the meetings, that last bite of food at the snack shop in the evening, and the fun at skit time where you ended up with a pie in the face—all of this is a part of camping.

Benefits for the Counselor

A camp counselor is someone who has the opportunity of discipling another person for a short period of time. There are many such relationships in the Bible which help us understand the process. Moses helped prepare Joshua for his future responsibilities, Barnabas spent time teaching Paul about the basics of the Christian faith and Paul in turn helped make Timothy a vital force in the early Church. A counselor is one who is used by God to help others grow and develop in their Christian walk.

As a person and a leader, you will grow, learn, make mistakes and profit from them. Far more important, you will have the satisfaction of knowing that you have been used as an instrument of God to help mold and develop the life of a child or young person. The experience of leading a person to a saving knowledge of Jesus Christ can never be surpassed by any other experience. To lead the camper to discover the Christian life, to assist him to grow and to help him find God's will for his life— these are experiences you will never forget.

Perhaps one day you will look back over your campers and will see another Joshua, Paul or Timothy. What a blessing it will be to know that God used you to help in the process. What joy and satisfaction you will experience!

Roles of the Counselor

What is a camp counselor? You are one who is in the position of giving an opinion, recommendation or advice for purpose or direction. You help and guide by word and deed. You have had a genuine experience with Jesus Christ and know the redeeming work of God in your life. You have a God-given love for children and young people and a genuine concern for their many problems. Two assets which are almost mandatory are the ability to camp and to counsel. The ability to counsel depends upon your interest in people. Because your main concern in camp is with people, you assume several roles.

Teacher

You are a teacher in the sense that your attitudes and actions are observed and either copied or reacted to by your campers. You are a teacher because you are involved in direct instruction. Campers realize that counselors are people and have faults. Therefore, they don't expect perfection. They will learn from you anyway, but they'll learn more if you admit that you know you're not perfect and show them that you try to improve. Your actions and attitudes toward others will teach with an impact. Your classroom is your dorm, the dinner table, the athletic field, the meeting hall and the chapel. Use it well!

Look for what is known as "teachable moments"—those situations and circumstances that can be used as object lessons to help bring out biblical truths. Jesus used them frequently as He walked along roads with His followers. He taught His disciples about God's love by His acceptance of people who came to Him, He used the large stones in a temple structure to reveal His Second Coming and He demonstrated the character of God by forgiving the woman caught in the act of adultery. These moments occurred during the normal course of Jesus' day and were transformed into helpful instruction about the nature of God. A good teacher uses whatever methods he has available and transforms them into learning activities for his students.

Friend

As a friend you are interested in each camper's likes and dislikes, his problems and his experiences. You accept him or learn to accept him for what he is. You are friendly, approachable and a good listener, but at the same time you avoid the danger of being too familiar. The camper learns to trust and to share his most intimate thoughts and fears when he knows that his confidence won't be broken. This relationship of a friend, however, exists on an adult-to-camper level. Campers don't respect the counselor who attempts to act on the camper's age level. Avoid the danger of being so "in" with the kids that they think of you as one of them and not as the leader. Campers do not want you to act as they do; you are an adult and as such should command their regard and respect. Establish yourself in their minds as a leader and your effectiveness will be greatly enhanced.

Administrator and Organizer

You may be involved in the actual running of the camp, helping with administrative duties if the need arises. This may involve anything from organizing and running an athletic program to assisting in the business office. It may also involve working with camper records and camp evaluation forms.

Your organizational skills will affect your relations with your campers. Many decisions are needed in the course of a camp experience and campers require someone to give them the direction necessary in order to make many of these decisions. Some campers will be able to develop their own organization for teams, cabin cleanup and problems that arise. But others will find it necessary to rely upon your advice and counsel. Organization displayed by the counselor comes in the form of suggestions and recommendations, questions and honest concern. In cases of planning for certain activities and functions, the campers can be encouraged to assume the responsibility for much of this. You can plan for the camp but you do not plan the camp.

Spiritual Leader

Have you ever considered yourself as a spiritual leader before? Needless to say, it may very well be a new role for you. You will minister to the needs of others instead of having others minister to you. This ministry of spiritual leadership is vital—it is the reason you are a counselor. In a sense, you'll be offering to the camper *your* spiritual strength. You will have to be under the control and direction of God and your ministry will involve praying with and for each of your campers. You will worship with them, search the Scriptures with them and attempt to answer their questions—or guide them to someone who can. You will be sharing God with the campers. By watching you, they will be able to see the Christian life in action.

Don't feel as though you are expected to be a perfect Christian. Most camp directors understand that you are feeling somewhat insecure and hesitant about your duties and responsibilities. Don't be afraid to ask some questions. Remember, your adequacy is in Christ, not your own resources. God desires for you to be a successful counselor too!

So counseling involves many jobs or roles, and camps and conferences will be only as effective as its counselors. Before you take the position, it is well to realize that the success of the conference in terms of human instrumentality will always rest with the counselor more than with any other person. It is through your personal interest, concern and friendliness that you will earn, in a very special way, the right, as well as the opportunity, to talk with a child or young person about his relationship with Jesus Christ. Speakers will be influential and used of God to provoke thought. Through their messages the Holy Spirit will work to bring conviction and a sense of need. But in most cases, you will be the one who discusses, questions, prays, presents and points out Scripture to the inquirer. You will also be the one who is involved in the direct follow-up program. This is a momentous responsibility but also a wonderful privilege.

Your value in the camping program cannot be overestimated. A speaker may fail to communicate, the program may be disorganized, but with good counselors, it will make little difference. You can make or break the camp and the camper.

A camp is not a vacation and anyone who uses a counseling experience for this purpose shouldn't attend. It's a job and a ministry. Your time is never your own; it belongs to your campers. There will be constant demands upon you as counseling is *very* strenuous and requires all of your resources.

Qualifications of a Camp Counselor

Well-qualified counselors are essential to a successful camp program. As you consider this wonderful area of ministry, ask yourself what your campers will see. No one expects you to be perfect but if you do not strive to excel in your position you will never be as effective as you could be. These qualifications set a high standard and it is our intention to help you become the best counselor possible.

The best qualifications are those of Christ Himself. His love, patience, poise, peace, strength, gentleness, insight and understanding of human nature are what you desire. As you grow in your day-by-day walk and relationship with Jesus Christ, these will be manifest more and more.

Modeling

The individual who teaches by example and is consistent enough to practice what he believes is a candidate for becoming a successful worker with pliable and impressionable campers. Your personal life, including philosophy, attitudes and beliefs, are constantly on trial and examination by the campers, camp staff, speakers, director and fellow counselors. Everything you are, say and do will be observed. Should your talk about your dates or behavior be heard by the campers? How do you react when your cabin loses a ball game? Respect is never demanded and gained but won and earned by the depth of your own personal life. Remember, more is caught than taught with youth.

What is the quality of your spiritual life? If you wait until camp to begin a regular and systematic devotional life, you will be unable to minister to your campers. Your relationship with Jesus Christ must be a constant, real, meaningful experience that is well established. Sincerity of convictions and adherence to the New Testament teachings on interpersonal relationships are qualities you should strive after. The real test of your spiritual life quite often comes into focus when problems arise in camp. This is where Christianity is real and can stand the test!

Knowledge of the Scriptures

Since many campers come to camp looking for answers to many of their questions, it will be a challenge for you to be able to relate biblical principles to their needs. The ability to pray before others, to defend your faith and to lead another person to Christ are but a few of the challenges that await you at camp.

You can prepare for your ministry by being consistent in your quiet time each day, making sure you are able to remember many of those verses you learned in your earlier days as a Christian.

Positive Attitude

Camp directors and staffs are constantly on the lookout for people with that quality called "being positive." A positive attitude is contagious, especially in camp. In a sense, you are really a salesman. You sell campers on everything—food, speakers, accommodations, program, athletics, crafts and your purpose for the camp. Even the presenting of Jesus Christ in a positive manner is important. And there is no other way in which to present Him!

Enthusiasm is one way of being positive, so be enthusiastic about the meetings, meals, recreational events, athletic competitions and cabin-inspection rivalries. When you ask questions positively, you'll get your campers in the habit of saying yes and you'll be surprised how this attitude catches on with the others.

Love

A counselor without the quality of love is not a counselor. Your love must have its basis in the love that God presented to you in Jesus Christ. Your love for others begins with your love for Him.

Your love must be displayed in very practical ways toward your campers. They'll know if it is real and genuine or manufactured. Kind words are readily accepted but without kind deeds, they are empty. Real patience, sympathy, empathy and understanding go hand in hand with love. Some children and adolescents aren't as easy to love as others and you may be repulsed because of physical deformities or personality disorders. Focus on a growing love.

Other campers will forever be getting into trouble and disrupting meetings and sleep! Some are overly verbal and are constantly talking. Then there are those who will never let you out of their sight. Some of these campers will attempt to "needle you" or "but you" constantly because you represent authority or because they don't like you. *Can you love these campers? You'll have to, for they are attending camp because of a need in their lives. You have the responsibility and challenge of trying to meet this need.* In many cases, they're more in need of love than the average individual in your group. This demands all the patience you can muster, but more than that, it requires a complete dependence upon Jesus Christ for the strength, insight and love that only He can give you.

Humility

Someone once said that the humble person is a much-sought-after but seldom found creature. His species is becoming extinct. Too many Christians today talk about having humility before God but fail to have any before man. As you counsel and talk with your group, talk about *their* lives, friends, education, hobbies and problems. Most people dislike hearing the person who cannot talk about anyone but himself. Campers tire of the counselor who attempts to impress or shock them by a constant barrage of personal experiences. Time is short and precious when you're at camp so use it well.

If you give any personal examples or experiences, don't be guilty of dragging out your past life before meeting Christ, as though you were proud of it. An example of this was evident one evening as a youth speaker told of his activities as a "hood and gangster" before becoming a Christian. Over two-thirds of the message was spent giving precise details of his notorious past associations and how he had never been caught and convicted. The last few moments of the message recalled his conversion experience and the change that had taken place in his life through the encounter he had with Jesus Christ. When the meeting ended several of the youth were heard to comment, "Man, he really lived it up, didn't he!"; "Hey, he sure lived quite the life before he became a Christian." Then one person asked the question, "I wonder why he got off without paying for any of those crimes? Is that the way it should be? It just doesn't seem right to me." The fact that this man met Christ and was a changed person didn't register with the audience because he had dwelt so much on his past. The attention-getters that we sometimes use can have a negative effect.

Personal Habits

Pleasing personal habits are very necessary in the close atmosphere of a camp. Tidiness with appearance, clothes and personal belongings do much to instill these same habits with your group. Do you clean up the area around your bunk and put things away? Getting to camp isn't an invitation to wear out all the old sloppy clothes that you have, nor is it an excuse to smell like the mules or horses that you ride. *Campers will imitate you.* They will pick up any bad habits you might exhibit. Are your table manners worth copying? If you're boisterous and use slang, complaining or boastful, unkempt and slovenly, expect the same to develop as you set the pattern!

Common Sense

Basic common sense is helpful to the counselor. It is almost essential to understand, guide and make adjustments to campers and the total camp program. If you have difficulty making decisions or knowing what *is* good common sense, or what *isn't*, then camp counseling can be a nightmare for you. Camps aren't looking for superior ratings when it comes to the intelligence factor, but they do want those who can make decisions and are sensible in their approach to everyday situations and problems.

Stable Character and Pleasant Personality

A stable character and pleasant personality are necessities if you are to command respect and be an example that others will emulate. One who attempts to understand opposing points of view is also a definite asset to the camping program. Some counselors have been more of a problem than the campers because of moodiness. You can't remain aloof in camp without affecting everyone and the total atmosphere of the camp. A real liking and interest in people and the enjoyment of being around them is something that each fledgling counselor must consider. If a negative reaction to this idea is present, camp counseling will be difficult. Camp life consists of living with people for 24 hours a day and no two campers are alike. Enjoy their uniqueness.

Honesty

Some positive camp experiences have actually been destroyed by a single counselor. This occurs when the counselor isn't aware of some shortcomings in his own life and creates more problems than is thought possible. Too many counselors come to camp conscious of some problems, personality deviations or uncontrollable habits, but are unwilling to do anything to correct them. If you fit into this category and are thinking of taking a position at a camp, whether it is for a summer or a weekend, disqualify yourself as a counselor and seek help. The one thing that you try to hide from others may be the same problem area one of your campers has. If he seeks you out and asks your help and advice, what will you be able to say or do? Honesty is a characteristic that is mandatory here. If a problem exists, be willing to admit it to yourself and to someone else who can assist you.

Emotional Maturity

Emotional maturity and stability are your close friends. Maintaining control at all times, carrying on a consistent relationship with other staff members, being self-confident and accepting and profiting from criticism—all of these behaviors exhibit emotional maturity.

If you are planning to counsel for an entire summer, this means leaving your family and friends, maybe your "steady," your favorite haunts and activities and your church. Can you be unaffected by absence from all of these? Do you have a nervous system that is able to stand the noise and stress of living with young, exuberant campers? Consider these before you undertake an extended counseling experience. If you decide to leave the camp during the middle of the season, you will affect the camp program and entire staff.

Reliability

Reliability is a very important quality that directors look for in a counselor. Running a camp is so much easier if the director can depend upon his staff, even when he isn't present. Counselors who are willing to abide by the rules that the camp has established are at a premium. The task of operating a camp involves work on the part of all staff members. Counselors who have a genuine interest in their work will cheerfully do more than what has been assigned to them. This involves working by yourself and with others. Mature counselors have the ability to sense and assume responsibility without having to be told everything.

Most camps have standards of behavior established not only for counselors but for the campers as well. The responsibility for seeing that all campers (not just your own) follow these standards falls upon you. This was pointed out in a camp situation where the effectiveness of the camp experience was almost totally ruined because some counselors failed to take responsibility. Several couples at this high school camp had become too affectionate and during the free time sat around in plain sight of everyone. Several counselors passed by but said, "Well, that's not my problem. They're not my campers. Their counselor ought to be around to see that!" And when confronted with this later the reply was, "Well, no one told me to handle that situation. It wasn't my responsibility. They have their own counselors." This is not the type of attitude that should prevail. Seek to maintain the standards of the camp with any and all campers.

Adaptability

Because a camp experience involves many people, situations arise which necessitate change. Camp directors seek out individuals who have the ability to adjust to new and varied situations and those who can accept responsibility for many tasks. The person who can work well with those who have "rough edges" on their personalities will contribute greatly to establishing a harmonious atmosphere among staff members.

Healthy

A sickly counselor is a hazard to those around him. Personal health standards are usually maintained by each camp, and counselors above all must have good health, seeking to maintain this while at camp. If you become ill or have an accident, seek out the camp nurse or physician immediately. This not only helps to ensure your health but is a strong motivating factor for campers to do the same. Health and safety consciousness is a standard that is continuous in its application.

It is also important to realize that your lack of concern for the basic health and safety needs of your campers could have an effect upon the entire camp by spreading germs and harmful bacteria. Don't allow your lack of personal discipline to ruin the week of camp for your campers.

Lack of sleep is one detriment to good health that you will face. Know your sleep requirement and attempt to meet it. But any attempt to compensate for lack of sleep must be done at a time when it doesn't hurt the camp program nor take you away from your duties.

Interest

Sincere interest in the outdoors and the camp where you are serving will enable you to maintain a proper attitude and perspective about your work. Some people love camping when the weather is bright and clear and the insects are a rarity, but can you maintain those same feelings about camp when it rains for two days and the mosquitoes make your sleep miserable? This is all a part of counseling and how you react to these problems will direct the reaction of your campers. Each camp and conference grounds is unique, having established traditions, goals and policies. You will do well to know and understand the traditions, ideals and objectives of the camp, the policies as they pertain to staff, camper relationships and operational standards, the procedures for beginning and closing camp, and the area immediately surrounding the camp.

Servanthood

Jesus gives us the best example of this essential quality. At camp you will become tired and in so doing will be tempted to try and take care of yourself first. Remember the example of Jesus, who considered others more important than Himself and then demonstrated this concern to those around Him. Look for ways to help your campers have the best camp experience possible.

These are just some of the qualities and characteristics that are sought after by the camp director. How do you measure up to these? Many years ago the results of a study indicated that certain characteristics tended to be identified with the better counselors. These qualities haven't changed throughout the years:

Executive ability and dispatch.
Ability to foresee consequences of conduct.
Ability and thoroughness in analyzing problems and situations.
Ability to formulate clearly specific objectives for campers.
Ability to get campers to propose, plan, initiate, execute and evaluate enterprises.
Ability to help campers face issues that arise in living together in the camp community.
Ability to use cooperative rather than autocratic methods of control.
Ability to extend and enlarge campers' interests.
Ability to deal intelligently with difficult campers.
Constructive participation in leaders' meetings.[1]

Campers, too, have had the opportunity to express themselves concerning the type of counselors that they favor. It is well to consider yourself from this perspective. At camp, you'll need to try to project yourself into the camper's situation and consider it from his viewpoint. See how he views you and what you say. Campers have stated that they like counselors who can be approached. In other words, they can talk with them and can get close to them. A friendly counselor is one who will be liked. Being agreeable (within limits) is another favorable trait along with being sympathetic and understanding. *Campers want counselors who are strict and can maintain order. There are times when you'd never believe this to hear them talk and complain, but inwardly they desire this type of leader.* Coupled with this, however, is the liking of a person who isn't unnecessarily severe, who isn't domineering and bossy and one who is fair and has no favorites in camp. They are also favorably inclined toward the person who participates in all of their activities with them.

How will you fit in as a counselor? Sounds a bit terrifying, doesn't it? And yet what a tremendous challenge! A weekend counseling at your own church camp or a week or even a summer at a conference center will permanently affect your life and will deepen your commitment to Jesus Christ.

Counselor Appraisal and Evaluation Forms

A good method of rating yourself as a prospective counselor has been presented in *Camp Counseling* by Viola Mitchell and Ida Crawford. These forms can be a valuable tool, not only for you, but for the camp and entire counseling staff. There are three methods of usage. First, you may use this as a guide to better understand yourself and strive for improvement in the weaker areas. Second, some camps keep the forms on file for the counselor to use during the camping season. The camp director can then discuss the results with the counselor.

The third method is perhaps the most beneficial. Small groups of counselors can meet together and share with one another how they rated themselves on the individual questions. Then the others in the group can tell the one who has just shared how they would rate him on the same form. Honest appraisal by others can be very helpful and revealing, but it takes a complete openness and a willingness to be objective about yourself.

If you would like to know your possibilities for success and enjoyment as a counselor, rate yourself on the tests which follow. You will be asked to evaluate yourself in two important areas of counseling preparedness: health and emotional maturity. Remember that there is nothing to be gained by cheating, for the real proof comes when you begin working with fellow staff members and campers on the job.

Check each trait in the proper column. Then connect them with a solid line to indicate your profile. Note where your weaknesses lie as the line slumps off to the left and also assess your strengths as the line bears triumphantly to the right.

Health Appraisal

	Poor 1	Below Average 2	Average 3	Above Average 4	Superior 5
1. Stamina enough to last through a strenuous day					
2. Well-balanced meals eaten regularly					
3. Regular sleep in sufficient quantity					
4. No smoking					
5. No intoxicating liquors					
6. Sufficient vigorous exercise each day					
7. Pleasing and neat appearance					
8. Cleanliness of person and clothing					
9. Graciousness and mannerliness					
10. Tact (speak truthfully, but without unnecessarily offending or hurting others)					
11. Cooperativeness (even when carrying out the plans of others)					
12. Cheerfulness (no sulking or moodiness)					
13. Sense of humor (even when the joke's on you)					
14. Good English (no profanity or excess slang)					

	Poor 1	Below Average 2	Average 3	Above Average 4	Superior 5
15. Warmth (a friendly personality that attracts others to you)					
16. Poise (even in emergencies or embarrassing situations)					
17. Appreciation of the beautiful in deed, music, nature and literature					
18. Sincere liking for campers (even unattractive and "naughty" ones)					
19. Enjoyment of hard work (even when it means getting your clothing dirty)					
20. Skills and knowledge of outdoor living (in rain, as well as sunshine)					
21. Adaptability (can happily change plans to fit in with others or the weather)					
22. Can take as well as give orders					
23. Love of fun (can see possibilities for enjoyment in almost any situation)					
24. Interested in many things					
25. Specialization (ability to do at least one camp activity well)					

	Poor 1	Below Average 2	Average 3	Above Average 4	Superior 5
26. Initiative (ability to start without outside prodding or suggestion)					
27. Promptness at all appointments and in performing all tasks					
28. Dependability (do what you say you will when you say you will)					
29. Industry (constantly up and doing)					
30. Persistence (finish what you start with dispatch and thoroughness)					
31. Curiosity (want to know about many things just for the sake of knowing)					
32. Neatness (keep own living quarters neat and clean)					

Emotional Maturity Appraisal

"When I was a child, I spoke as a child, . . . but when I became a man, I put away childish things" (1 Cor. 13:11, *NKJV*) is not necessarily true of all adults. A person who harbors childish traits is said to be emotionally immature, and, though frequently at a loss to understand why, he is often unhappy, for his behavior keeps him at constant odds with himself and his associates. He often feels mistreated and deprived of his just dues. Camp directors look upon a counselor's degree of emotional maturity as one of the surest indices of his probable success. You can scarcely expect to fulfill your job of helping your campers mature unless you can set an example.

Your physical and mental maturity tell nothing of your emotional maturity. The fact that you are strong as an ox or fleet as a deer does not indicate that you have learned to face up to life squarely and solve your problems in an adult way. Indeed, you may be a straight *A* student at school and still be unable to apply any of your intelligence to solve your own problems and help you deal more effectively with people.

How often we hear some exasperated person say to another, "Why don't you grow up?" What actions and attitudes determine maturity? Why is one person labeled mature and another immature? First of all, a mature person has awakened to the fact that every person around him has wants and needs similar to his own and he therefore cannot always have his own way. For instance, if you have set your heart on doing something with a particular friend on your day off, you don't sulk, try to get even, or throw a tantrum if you find they have made other plans or that unforeseen developments have made it necessary for one of you to remain on duty in camp. You try to persuade others to your way of thinking but you do it by reasoning with them, not by pouting, wheedling, flattering or making yourself so disagreeable that others give in rather than suffer the consequences.

When someone with obviously good intentions criticizes something about you, you are smart enough to analyze the remark and profit by any truth there is in it, instead of flaring up pigheadedly at the thought that another should even hint that you are anything less than perfect. You have pride and faith in yourself yet display a becoming modesty and don't feel it necessary to alibi for every shortcoming. You aren't a doormat who lets everyone walk over you at will; you may even on occasion rise up in righteous anger or resentment about things important enough to really matter.

You enjoy the feeling of being able to influence others but don't misuse this ability. You exercise it only to lead in right directions but avoid carrying it to the point where you make willing slaves of others and have them groveling at your feet. You don't try to run people's lives but, instead, try to do a good job of running your own. You organize your daily living with a good balance of work, play, laughter, seriousness and all other components of the good life. You can fit easily into the routine of camp living, accepting reasonable camp rules cheerfully, because you know they are meant to protect the best interests of all. Most of all, you are thoughtful of others and considerate of their needs and wishes.

The real criterion is that the emotionally immature person governs his actions by his emotions whereas the mature person keeps his reasoning power instead of his emotions in the driver's seat at all times.

In order to make a rough estimate of your overall emotional maturity, total all scores and divide by 25 (the number of items rated). If you have proceeded honestly and objectively, an average of four or five means you are quite acceptable, three indicates you are average, and a one or two shows that you are below average and should "grow up." Here are some suggestions to help you attain emotional maturity:

1. Face your deficiencies frankly, and resolve to eradicate them just as quickly and completely as possible.

2. Set out to acquire definite skills and interests which have social rather than selfish or personal values.

3. Make it a point to associate with a number of emotionally mature people. Observe them and try to determine why they are so.[2]

Emotional Maturity

	Poor 1	Below Average 2	Average 3	Above Average 4	Superior 5
1. Can you accept criticism without undue anger or hurt, acting upon it if justified, disregarding it if not?					
2. Are you tolerant of others and willing to overlook their faults?					
3. Do you feel genuinely happy at the success of others and sincerely congratulate them?					
4. Do you refrain from listening to and repeating undue gossip about others?					
5. Do you converse about other things and persons? Test it by checking your conversation to see how frequently you use the pronoun "I."					
6. Are you altruistic, often putting the welfare and happiness of others above your own?					
7. Do you refrain from emotional outbursts of anger, tears, etc.?					
8. Do you face disagreeable duties promptly and without trying to escape by playing sick or making excuses?					
9. Can you stay away from home a month or more without homesickness?					

	Poor 1	Below Average 2	Average 3	Above Average 4	Superior 5
10. Can you weigh facts and make decisions promptly, then abide by your decisions?					
11. Are you willing to postpone things you want to do now in favor of greater benefits or pleasure later?					
12. Are you usually on good terms with your family and associates?					
13. When things go wrong, can you objectively determine the cause and remedy it without alibiing for yourself and blaming it on other people or things?					
14. When disagreeing with another, can you discuss it calmly and usually work out a mutually satisfactory agreement without hard feelings?					
15. Can you enter into informal social events of many types wholeheartedly?					
16. Do you really enjoy doing little things for others, even though you know they will likely go unknown and unappreciated?					
17. Do you dress neatly and modestly without tendency to gaudiness or overdress?					

	Poor 1	Below Average 2	Average 3	Above Average 4	Superior 5
18. Can you dismiss past sins and mistakes that can't be remedied now without dwelling on them?					
19. Can you make decisions regarding others objectively, disregarding your personal dislike or resentment of them?					
20. As a leader, do you work democratically without dictating or forcing your will on others?					
21. Are you loyal to your friends, minimizing or not mentioning their faults to others?					
22. Are you free from "touchiness," so that others do not have to handle you with kid gloves?					
23. Do you act according to your honest convictions regardless of what others may think or say about it?					
24. Do you have a kindly feeling toward most people, a deep affection for some, and no unhealthy attachments to any?					
25. Do you feel that you usually get about what you deserve? Are you free from a feeling that others "have it in for" you?					

4. If you feel a need for help, seek someone qualified and discuss the problem frankly and openly with him. Be willing to act on his recommendations even though they're not flattering.

5. Get wrapped up in causes so big and worthwhile that they completely absorb you, making you forget yourself and your troubles.

Ask Key Questions

Before you begin your counseling at a camp, whether it be for a weekend, week or entire summer, you should know something about the camp and what is expected of you. These are questions to ask yourself about your position:

1. Is a job description available so I may know what is expected of me?

2. Do I know what this camp is like in its physical facilities, layout and camp boundaries?

3. Do I know how the camp is organized, the line of command or staff relationships?

4. Have the camp objectives been clarified and am I in agreement with them?

5. What are my responsibilities to the campers, other staff members, director and church (if counseling for a particular church)?

6. What free time do I have at camp and what provisions are made for personal use of the equipment?

7. Am I insured? What are the arrangements for friends or family who may come to visit? If I am to be paid, what is the amount and when?

8. Who is my immediate superior?

9. What age group will I be counseling and will any information be made available concerning the campers' backgrounds?

10. Are there any records or reports that I'll be required to keep?

11. Are Bible study and follow-up materials available to me from the camp itself or am I to bring my own?

12. What are the standards the camp expects me to maintain?

13. What type of follow-up program does this camp use and will I be able to carry this out?

14. Will the camp train me in areas in which I am weak and inexperienced?

Questions for Further Discussion

1. What qualifications did Jesus possess that helped make Him such an effective counselor?
2. What are the characteristics of Jesus' life-style that made people want to get to know Him?
3. Review the 15 counselor qualities presented in this chapter. Of those presented, which ones are a present strength for you? Which are present weaknesses?
4. What can you do between now and the beginning of camp to help strengthen a weak quality?
5. Review the health appraisal form. Which qualities are your strongest? Which ones are your weakest?
6. What can you do between now and the beginning of camp to strengthen a weak area?
7. Based on the emotional maturity appraisal form, what area do you need to improve between now and the beginning of camp?
8. How will you improve this area specifically?

3
Camping as a Team Ministry

Several years ago the afternoon train pulled into a small Quaker town in Pennsylvania and a stranger alighted. He walked over to one of the people on the platform and said, "What type of town is this and what kind of people live here?"

"What kind of place did you come from and what were the people like who lived there?" the Quaker replied.

"They were hard people to get along with and the town was noisy."

"This is the same kind of town and the same kind of people." The stranger got back on the train.

The next afternoon when the train pulled in, off hopped another stranger. Smiling, he approached the group on the platform and cheerily said, "Hi, there! I'm looking for a town to live in permanently. What do you have here?"

Once more the Quaker replied, "Where did you come from and what were the people like?"

"I came from a happy place and the people were kind and friendly."

"You'll find the same conditions here," said the Quaker.

"Good! I need a place like this to live. Will you help me get settled?"

"Sure!" chorused the group.

Your attitudes are an indication of what you may expect in others. Knowing when and how to give is the secret of getting along with other people.

Getting along with others and working harmoniously with them is going to be your responsibility while at camp. Interpersonal relationships among counselors and other staff members influence camp morale.

Organizational Models

There are many different types and styles of camps across America. Each has a unique program based upon a distinct philosophy of camping. In order to help you understand what type of camp you may be counseling at and who you should see for help, several models of camps, also known as organizational charts, will be displayed. As you see the manner in which your camp operates you will perhaps be able to identify the type of camp at which you are counseling. That will assist you in your understanding of how the camp runs and who is in charge of what areas of responsibility.

Each organizational model is based upon a different philosophy of camping. Some prefer to divide the campers into smaller groups and maintain those groups for all of the camp activities (i.e. sleeping, eating, games, etc.). Other camps prefer larger groups which require more staff and departmentalization. These larger camps house the campers in dormitories and allow campers the freedom to choose their recreational options, where they sit in the dining hall and which meetings to attend. Each camp has its own distinct way of operating and knowing which style of camp you are going to be counseling in will help you understand why they do certain things and perhaps who to speak with when you have a problem. The responsibilities of staff members and counselors vary greatly with each style of camp. At a large camp you may never see the camp director; at a small camp he may be helping out in the kitchen during meal-

The Conference Camp

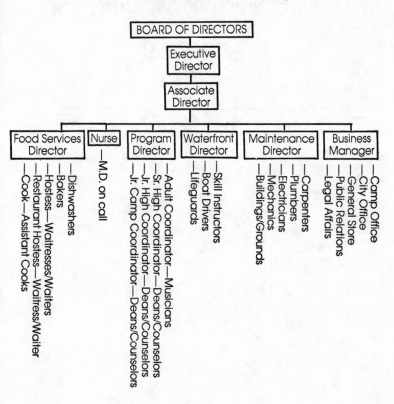

BOARD OF DIRECTORS

Executive Director

Associate Director

Food Services Director
—Cook—Assistant Cooks
—Restaurant Hostess—Waitress/Waiter
—Hostess—Waitresses/Waiters
—Bakers
—Dishwashers

Nurse
—M.D. on call

Program Director
—Jr. Camp Coordinator—Deans/Counselors
—Jr. High Coordinator—Deans/Counselors
—Sr. High Coordinator—Deans/Counselors
—Adult Coordinator—Musicians

Waterfront Director
—Lifeguards
—Boat Drivers
—Skill Instructors

Maintenance Director
—Buildings/Grounds
—Mechanics
—Electricians
—Plumbers
—Carpenters

Business Manager
—Legal Affairs
—Public Relations
—General Store
—City Office
—Camp Office

Model 1

Medium Camp (100-300 Campers)

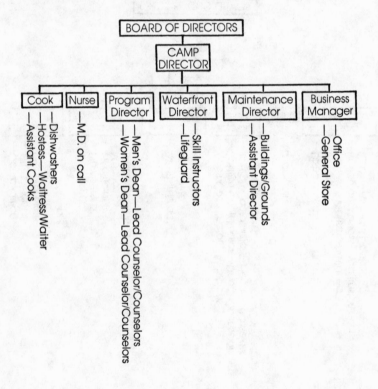

Model 2

Small Camp (1-100 Campers)

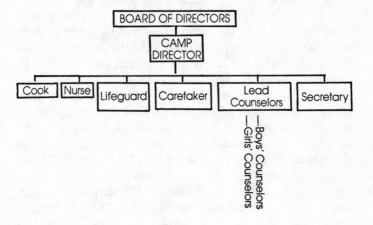

Model 3

time. But, no matter where he is, be assured that he wants you to perform to the best of your abilities and to be happy.

The Camp Director

If you think you do an unlimited amount of work at camp, take over the job of camp director for a season and you'll find out what work really is! The camp director usually spends many weeks and months in advance preparation. He is responsible for the entire camp and is concerned with each person—whether he be dishwasher, counselor, camper, speaker or maintenance worker. His job is complex and momentous, and he has more problems and responsibilities than you have ever thought possible. The last problem he wants is a difficult counselor. In a sense, *your* job is to make *his* job easier by carrying out your duties to the fullest and not creating any additional work. Loyalty to the camp director is expected of all staff workers.

If there is a difference of opinion concerning camp policies and the manner in which things are done, go straight to the camp director and talk to him about the problem. He will appreciate a direct approach rather than hearing about it through the grapevine. It is easy to be critical of rules and regulations but sometimes difficult to carry them out in a spirit of cheerfulness and understanding. Don't ask for special favors. Standards and consistent decisions are an important factor in maintaining good morale.

You have been asked to be a counselor because you have the ability to make decisions and to deal with problems. There will be occasions when you'll wonder whether to tackle a problem or ask for help and assistance. Any minor difficulties should be handled by you but those that take special training and advice might be out of your jurisdiction. Quite often, a camp will have a men's dean and a women's dean or a program director in charge of counselors. These are the people to seek out first instead of going directly to the camp director. If they are unable to assist, they will say so and have you then contact the director.

Camp directors expect counselors to be efficient, prompt, enthusiastic, cooperative, capable of handling work, prompt in turning in all reports and well trained for the specific job assigned to them. They also expect counselors to exhibit conduct in all situations outside the camp that will reflect well on the camp.

Since the camp director is involved with the details of operating the camp, it is difficult for him to do that plus see that campers are getting the best experience they can receive. For this reason many camps have a program director. He is an essential part of any large camp or conference center.

The Program Director

The duties of the program director will vary depending on the style and size of the camp or conference center. At larger camps he ensures the continuity of camp programs among all the different age-group camps, e.g. juniors, junior highers, senior highers and adults. At medium-sized camps, which have one program, he will be responsible for the quality of the camp program.

He may be the one who teaches the counselor training sessions, supervises the men's and women's deans, oversees the waterfront director and coordinates the level of skill development at the camp. He may also be the one that handles the difficult discipline problems at camp such as drinking, drugs, fighting, sex and smoking. It is a demanding job which requires long hours. He should be a good administrator and counselor himself. Anything that affects the camper usually goes through the program director first. If you have a problem as a counselor, he is probably the one to look for to get a solution.

Your Fellow Counselors

The quality of the camp staff will determine the camp morale. If tensions and animosities exist between counselors, campers will be swift to perceive this and, in some cases, capitalize upon the fact. You will have to work at fitting into the group, and, in some instances, go out of your way to establish new friendships.

Don't wait for the other counselors to make the first approach; be outgoing with all fellow workers. Friendliness can be contagious. Most of us, however, wait to catch it from someone else instead of giving the others the opportunity to catch it from us. Don't wait around to see if people will like you; just assume that they will. Don't wait for them to be the first to say hello or to smile. Take the lead, be friendly and they will follow. If everyone waits around for someone to make the first overture, the atmosphere can become very uncomfortable and cool. People relax when others put themselves out by breaking the ice. But be careful: cliques and special favorites among counselors can have a dire effect upon everyone. Total involvement will be more advantageous to you and the entire group.

Gossip and chance comments have a way of filtering back to the person involved. By the time they arrive, they're usually distorted and even worse than when first said. How would you react if you picked up the information that another counselor had slandered you? You would probably feel like retaliating and this would then add fuel to the fire, perhaps exploding in a disruptive way and affecting the outcome of the camp! If you have a grievance against someone and are unable to understand him, try to see things from his viewpoint. Pray about the problem and the person. Then talk with him directly! If the situation still exists, ask for assistance from your supervisor.

If you have a complaint concerning the quality of work done by others, be sure that yours is above reproach! Forget the remarks you hear about other staff members. Encourage the speaker to solve the problem by other means. Remember, though, that you can't solve all problems by yourself. A regular, meaningful prayer life helps overcome seemingly insurmountable difficulties.

Privacy is a rarity at camp and the private moments that you will have are cherished. Be sure to consider the privacy of others, not only the individual but also his property and belongings. It is the best policy not to borrow or lend personal articles, clothing or money. Towns and supply stores are close at hand.

A counseling staff that cooperates with one another, is unselfish in interest and work, exhibits patience, tact, friendliness, loyalty and open-mindedness will see the results in the quality of the camp and the lives of the campers. Set aside some time during the week when you and the other counselors can get together for Bible study, prayer and a sharing of problems.

Perhaps you've had some experience counseling. If so, you can be a tremendous asset to the novice. You know the administrative policies and routines of camp. You may have special techniques that have aided you in handling campers. Sharing of your experiences in a helpful and humble way can save hours of frustration for the new counselor.

Don't hesitate to give credit, appreciation and encouragement. If someone is deserving of a compliment, give it to him. In fact, go out of your way to do so. Too many people are tight-lipped with their words of praise. It isn't difficult to find an achievement that merits praise. If you look for the little things, instead of the big ostentatious feats, you'll find much more to commend a person. Many people are uncertain about themselves and you may give them the reassurance they need. Encouragement, patience, a willingness to listen, praise when deserved and small constructive doses of criticism will help this new fellow worker.

There is no place in the camping program for sarcasm or harassment. New counselors may be inept or ineffective at times, but they can learn if given the opportunity and encouragement. Include all your colleagues in discussions and decisions.

If you are a new counselor, don't hesitate to consult the experienced person. But avoid the danger of becoming overly dependent.

Realize also that visits by friends from home are subject to the policy of the camp. They can be seen on your time off. Usually they have to seek accommodations away from camp.

Another area of concern is that of boy-girl relationships. Each camp will have its own policy concerning dating activities between women and men counselors. Any relationships here set an example for the entire camp. You will be carefully observed and discussed by the campers! Frequent upsets between counselors who are going together can hamper testimony and effectiveness. Be careful of matchmaking between counselors.

Campers quickly pick this up and soon the information, whether true or not, is spread throughout the entire camp. At no time should you date campers. Guys will counsel guys and girls will counsel girls. Rarely, if ever, should a guy counselor counsel a girl camper, and vice versa.

The Counselor's Job Description

The responsibilities you have as a camp counselor will depend on the style and size of the camp you attend. At a conference-style camp your duties will be to ensure that the campers are at all of the meals, meetings and other important events. You will be required to conduct an evening Bible study or devotional in the cabin before going to sleep. Freeing you up from routine activities so you are able to establish meaningful relationships with your campers is a common philosophy. It is on the basis of this relationship that campers will often respond in a meeting.

At a medium-sized or smaller camp your duties may include the above but also quite a bit more. You may be expected to teach a particular skill such as archery, canoeing, volleyball, hiking, etc. You may also be asked to teach a morning and/or evening Bible study for your campers. It is even possible that you may be asked to assist in the snack shack in the afternoon and help with the dishes after the meals.

There is much to be done at a camp and the counselor who helps out willingly is the one who is most appreciated. Enter into your duties, regardless of what they are, with an attitude of servanthood and humility.

One way to initiate good interpersonal relationships with your campers is to start out on the right foot. Greet the campers in a friendly manner and let them know that you are happy they'll be in your cabin. Show that you are interested in them and what they like, perhaps by asking questions. Be sure to learn their names as soon as possible.

Perhaps it is a real climb up the hill to the cabins. Don't be one of those who stands and laughs at the pathetic struggle of some camper as he attempts to tote, drag, push or even roll his belongings toward his home for the week. Ask if you can help, but don't jump in and grab the gear. He may prefer doing it his way, regardless of how it looks to you.

Let the campers know the schedule, camp procedure and necessary rules concerning all phases of camp life. Then let them ask questions. Use some of the experienced campers to help orient the novices, but work closely with them so they learn how to do this properly. Let the campers discuss with you what they are seeking at camp and what they like to do. This will certainly aid you as you work with them.

Participate in all camp activities—from K.P. to devotions, from cleaning the dorm to playing a game of softball. In lieu of ordering the campers to follow established rules, work and play with them to show them the routine and framework of camp. Joining the campers on an assignment or work project is much more effective than telling them.

Although facilities are there for the enjoyment and use of campers and counselors, most camps indicate that campers should have the first opportunity to use them. This includes the swimming pool, tennis, volleyball and basketball courts, baseball diamonds, Ping-Pong tables and arts and crafts supplies. You may use them when it doesn't interfere with the campers although you'll have ample time to participate in all of these activities with the campers. Some camps also set aside a brief time each day for just the staff to use one facility.

As you work with your campers and observe other counselors, you'll notice that the wise counselor avoids personal arguments and emotional involvements with campers. Some campers find it difficult not to step out of bounds now and then, even though you are the symbol of authority in their eyes. They may even break a rule just to see how you will react! Correction should come quickly and quietly, then the matter should be dropped.

Establishing Meaningful Relationships

Although there is an art to establishing meaningful relationships, the following checklist will prove to be practical and encouraging to the camp counselor:

1. Have a genuine liking for people. If you don't, please don't consider the field of counseling. You have to be interested in people and in finding their good points.

2. Be able to share with others—your knowledge, strength, relationship with God—everything that would help another individual.

3. Use the "we attitude" and be a cooperator. The camp is more interested in achieving its goals and objectives than in knowing who accomplished what! Be sure ideas are presented and the job is accomplished—whether you get the credit or not.

4. Learn from your mistakes and instead of calling them blunders or failures, consider them an education. The difference between a successful and unsuccessful person is this: the former doesn't make the same mistake twice.

5. Be decisive and don't wait too long to make decisions. Have a sense of confidence.

6. Have some ability to compromise when the circumstances warrant it, but never compromise on camp standards and policies.

7. When you are wrong, admit it. If you've made a mistake that affects others, apologize.

As you serve your church or camp as a counselor, and as you gain experience over the years, you will be given added responsibilities. There will be occasions when you will have to reprimand and constructively criticize others. This may involve campers or other counselors who work with and under your supervision. You'll need a peculiar ability to deal with others without giving offense—in other words, tact! When you must criticize, make sure you criticize *the act* and not *the person*. This makes the individual feel less insecure and skeptical, and he finds it much easier to accept your advice. Never criticize when you are angry, for if you let your emotions run away with your senses, your remarks will be regretted. Maintain and adopt a constructive attitude, remembering that the purpose of criticism is to help others improve and be a better counselor. Criticism is an educational process, so make it constructive. Sarcasm has no place in criticism and will leave scars that take years to heal.

Whenever a mistake is made, it doesn't always mean that just one person was at fault. Someone else might be involved and that someone may be you! Quite often others fail to carry out orders and duties because of a counselor's faulty, unclear instructions.

If you've ever been criticized in public, you know what a humiliating experience it is. One seems to lose his self-respect, becoming bitter and resentful. Any and all criticism should come in private.

Our final suggestion has been labeled the "sandwich" method of criticism. This involves slipping your criticism or suggestions for improvement in between two layers of compliments. The compliments should be sincere and if so, you'll find a receptive listener.

There could be suggestions and more suggestions on how to work with others—and yet how important it is that you be able to work well with people. The finest suggestions, helps and admonitions were penned by the apostle Paul: "Be humble and gentle. Be patient with each other, making allowance for each other's faults because of your love. Try always to be led along together by the Holy Spirit, and so be at peace with one another. We are all parts of one body, we have the same Spirit, and we have all been called to the same glorious future" (Eph. 4:2-4, *TLB*).

"Don't use bad language. Say only what is good and helpful to those you are talking to, and what will give them a blessing. Don't cause the Holy Spirit sorrow by the way you live. Remember, he is the one who marks you to be present on that day when salvation from sin will be complete. Stop being mean, bad-tempered and angry. Quarreling, harsh words, and dislike of others should have no place in your lives. Instead, be kind to each other, tenderhearted, forgiving one another, just as God has forgiven you because you belong to Christ" (Eph. 4:29-32, *TLB*).

"In everything you do, stay away from complaining and arguing" (Phil. 2:14, *TLB*).

"You are living a brand new kind of life that is continually learning more and more of what is right, and trying constantly to be more and more like Christ who created this new life within you. In this new life one's nationality or race or education or social position is unimportant; such things mean nothing. Whether a person has Christ is what matters, and he is equally available to all. Since you have been chosen by God who has given you a new kind of life, and because of his deep love and concern for you, you should practice tenderhearted mercy and kindness to others. Don't worry about making a good impression on them but be ready to suffer quietly and patiently. Be gentle and ready to forgive; never hold grudges. Remember, the Lord forgave you, so you must forgive others. Most of all, let love guide your life, for then the whole church will stay together in perfect harmony. Let the peace of heart which comes from Christ be always present in your hearts and lives, for this is your responsibility and privilege as members of his body. And always be thankful. Remember what Christ taught and let his words enrich your lives and make you wise; teach them to each other and sing them out in psalms and hymns and spiritual songs, singing to the Lord with thankful hearts" (Col. 3:10-16, *TLB*).

Questions for Further Discussion

1. Why is a camp program seen as a team ministry?
2. Read 1 Corinthians 12:12-27. What does this passage of Scripture teach regarding the importance of a team ministry for a Christian camp?
3. How can the poor performance of a camp counselor hinder the effectiveness of the camp director?
4. What are the advantages and disadvantages of a large, conference-style camp?
5. What are the advantages and disadvantages of a medium-sized or smaller camp?
6. Why is communication so important in a camp's operation? How can poor communication weaken the ministry of a camp program?
7. What will you do when a camper breaks a rule just to see how you will respond?

8. Can you identify the style of camp at which you will be counseling? Have you received your counseling responsibilities in writing? Have you discussed the details of your responsibilities with your lead counselor, program director or camp director?

4
Understanding
the Camper

The age-group characteristics presented in this chapter will help you understand and remember what it was like being a particular age. It may have been a while since you were a junior higher, and longer since being a junior. As you read through this chapter, try and remember what you were like at each age level. You will ask yourself many times while observing the behavior of a junior, junior higher or senior higher, *Was I really like that?* Or you'll be tempted to think, *I was never that hard to get along with, was I?* Chances are you were—but you won't remember it! It will be helpful to you to know what is normal and expected behavior, even when it is wrong, and what is not normal or expected. It will give you a basis for discipline, counsel and guidance.

The Junior Camper
(Ages 9-11)

Physically

The junior camper is a bundle of energy. He is very active and just loves to do things. He doesn't walk from place to place—he runs. He plays, wrestles, dives around the room or recreation area and is constantly on the go. *Do* is the word for the junior. He is strong and healthy at this age and the suscepti- bility of early childhood diseases is passing. The smaller muscles are developing so he still needs proper food, rest and supervi- sion. The growth rate is slowed and he is beginning to fill out. Girls at this age are sometimes taller than the fellows. The junior camper really loves the out-of-doors and doesn't like to feel penned in. This is the time for adventure and hiking, horse- back riding, hunting and fishing. He likes the difficult and com- petitive and notices the accomplishments of others. If he is interested enough and challenged, he will practice constantly to accomplish his goal. He has the tendency to make a sharp dis- tinction between work and play.

Suggestions: Provide a variety of constructive things for him to do and let him choose those activities that appeal to him the most. Develop leadership ability and responsibility by pro- viding the proper training situations for him. Challenge his ability with projects and games. Make a game out of the work projects. Do things *with* him and not *for* him. But be aware of the individ- ual who tires easily and see to it that he gets enough sleep and relaxation.

Because he admires strength and power, you can show the junior camper how God enabled men and women in the Bible to be strong and to do His will. Show how he, too, can be strong in his own Christian life.

Mentally

At this stage, the junior has many interests. Anything new holds a fascination for him. He is inquisitive and wants to know why and what makes things tick. He likes to read and he may not be too selective in his reading material. He enjoys history and geography and is developing a great interest in facts. His ability to memorize is very sharp and he has great capacity for reten- tion. He's a collector and keeps things because of the material itself or for some future use.

This is an age of realism and he enjoys real-life stories. He is an imitator, draws general conclusions and is beginning to understand relationships. He is beginning to comprehend how things and events fit together. At times, he can be quick to jump to conclusions so care must be exercised to point out all sides to him. His attention span is lengthening and can be from 20 to 40 minutes. Sometimes he can be interested in a project for an entire day, but when he drops it, he may drop it completely.

Suggestions: Capitalize on his wide variety of interests and encourage him not only to ask but to answer some of his own questions. This can be the ideal time to stimulate his desire to know God and His plan of salvation. This is the age to teach him about the chronology, history and geography of the Bible and God's wonderful creation.

His collecting ability can be a source of enjoyment, not only to himself, but to others, and there are many objects at camp that can be used to help him begin a hobby.

His curiosity can be directed to discover why people act the way they do and how God deals with them. This can lead into a discussion of his own relationship with Christ.

Help him to acquire good reading material, especially when he returns home. Christian fiction, biography, Bible storybooks and especially the Bible are materials he needs. You may have a library or bookstore at camp and your guidance here may instill some values for future selections. Present the Scripture as the Word of God and deal immediately with some of his problems—showing him the answers. This will encourage him to continue reading the Bible and to memorize helpful passages.

Socially and Emotionally

He can accept some responsibility, but he doesn't like authority over him, for he is striving to become more independent. He does, however, respect authority and wants limits. The gang stage is present here and the leadership within the gang shifts according to the activity. His friends are sought out from within his own age group and he favors his own sex.

Within the past few years, the juniors have been paying more attention to the opposite sex than ever before and in some communities and schools, dating activities are even encouraged! Because of this, we occasionally run into a youngster who is quite interested in the opposite sex. For the most part, however, there still exists some good-natured antagonism between boys and girls. The boys naturally think of themselves as being bigger, braver and stronger.

Juniors are very proud of newly acquired skills and lack patience with younger children who can't do as they can. Teamwork is also important and so are contests. Ball games and any other competitions are the vogue for these youngsters. They are hero worshipers, are very conscious of their own abilities and enjoy telling about past deeds and exploits. Fairness and honesty are important to them and they usually give in proportion to what they receive. Any recognition they can elicit from you is gratifying.

Their frankness may sometimes surprise you. Be alert to discern the truth in what they tell, as exaggeration can be very common. The traits that children criticize most in others are attention-getting behaviors: fighting, bossiness, grouchiness and not being helpful to others.

Emotionally, they have just a few fears at this age but the present-day pressures are ever increasing. There are the pressures from society, the threat of all-out war, the continual barrage of advertising and the desire to succeed academically and socially. All of these pressures have increased over the years and the effect can be evidenced in some of the distorted and disrupted lives you will find. Knowing the environmental background of your campers will aid you in your counsel. Quick temper is a problem; they tend to flare up in a moment's notice. Any outward displays of affection are generally repulsed, especially by the boys. A well-developed sense of humor characterizes this group and adds to the delightfulness of working with them.

Suggestions: He will respond to you much more if you act as a guide and not a dictator. When you present plans, do it enthusiastically and use the "let's do" approach. If he can see the advantages of complete participation and cooperation, he will go along with it. He will participate if he feels that he is cooperating rather than submitting. He can be challenged to use his leadership ability for God right there at camp—then at home and school. If he realizes it is a rewarding experience to serve God in a wholehearted manner, he will. Camp projects and activities requiring teamwork and competition will be satisfying. Structure projects and games so he is able to achieve satisfying results because he becomes discouraged by failure. Scripture can be used to show how a Christian should act toward others and how to become an effective witness.

The junior's desire to achieve can be directed toward the areas of Bible memorization, helping around the camp and participation in camp services and camp fires. He may find it easy to live the Christian life here at camp, but you will have to challenge and prepare him to live for Christ when he returns home.

Give him specific examples of what he can do for and with others. Capitalize on his hero worship stage by providing him with Christian heroes he can look up to and emulate. Well-known Christians in various fields such as science, sports, school and missionary work will show him that Christians can be outstanding and find wonderful opportunities in their vocation. Heroes from the Old and New Testament should also be among those that he seeks after. But Jesus Christ should be at the center of his life—as far as following any one person is concerned! Your own example will speak louder than anything you happen to say so watch your step.

Opportunity for developing sportsmanship is an area that will be a challenge. He plays and competes to win and often finds it hard to accept failure and defeat. Help him face failure and learn to derive value from an activity itself without having to win to receive any benefit.

Any fears that he may have can be discussed and evaluated. There are some things to fear and there are other fears that are unfounded. Here, as everywhere else, the appropriate Scriptures should be presented.

Spiritually

It is very difficult to distinguish spiritual characteristics from the others; the spiritual area of a person's life cannot be divorced from the other aspects. Many applications have already been made to this, but a few facts here may complete the picture. A junior camper can understand Bible doctrine now and knows what sin and salvation are. In fact, this is one of the peak ages for commitments to Christ. Naturally, a real effort should be made to present the person of Jesus Christ, who is able to take away all sin. But juniors won't completely grasp symbolism and don't really appreciate it, either. Object lessons at camp should be selected carefully or they will never get the point.

Suggestions: Do not use abstract illustrations or talk about issues that are difficult to describe and explain such as the Trinity, eschatology, charismatic gifts, etc. Try and keep to the essential doctrines such as God's love, forgiveness, omnipotence, etc. These are reassuring to a junior and won't confuse him. Any issue involving abstract or complex concepts should be taught at a later age. Keep to the basics with junior children and you'll do well.

He will raise pertinent questions about Christianity and your answers should be truthful as well as scripturally based. If you don't know the answer, admit it and attempt to find out. Standards can be high and you can help him to meet them, but be sure the standards are realistic and biblically based. Whatever you do, avoid emotional appeals in presenting Christ to this age group.

It is not surprising that junior campers are extremely receptive to the gospel and very open to becoming a Christian. Counselors frequently have to deal with a junior's conversion due to their depth of trust and simplicity of faith. It is unfortunate, however, that many end up making a decision for Christ again when they reach junior or senior high. They often state that they did not know what they were doing earlier. Therefore, be sure you spend time explaining this important decision with them *before* they make it. Don't be in a hurry to "get another one"; rather, be sure they understand the implications of their commitment.

The Junior High Camper
(Ages 12-14)

This age has been labeled the "mixed-up" age, the "time of turbulence" or the "goof-off" stage. But no matter what you call it, it is an age of transition.

Physically

The junior higher readily responds to action, for this is a period of rapid and sometimes uneven growth, with an abundance of energy. He may appear to be as strong (and sometimes as big!) as an adult, but awkward as a newborn colt. The junior higher feels increased energy and strength, but hates to admit that he is tired or should slow his pace. Girls are physically ahead of the boys. This is the time of puberty and there are definite physical changes taking place in both sexes.

Suggestions: As his counselor, you are responsible for him; even guiding in matters of proper food, rest and exercise. Participation in games that allow him to use most of his muscles are best, but he also needs to be guided to some of the less energetic activities at camp, such as crafts. This is an important time for establishing the proper care of one's body and to emphasize that God created man in this way for a particular purpose. He can realize that his body is a temple of the Holy Spirit and he needs to care for and govern it according to the way God has set forth. Activities and habits that are harmful to the physical growth of a person, such as the intake of drugs, tobacco and alcohol, can be discussed in light of the Scriptures. You can also be sure that he will have many questions concerning some of the changes taking place in his body.

Mentally

At this time, the junior high camper is nearing the adult level of mental capacity. There is a greater ability to exercise reason and judgment, and he will if given the proper conditions and opportunity. He likes to use his imagination and investigate. If real life lacks stimulation he can retreat into a world of fantasy and satisfy his needs somewhat. However, if life can be made enjoyable and meaningful enough for him, this is the much more suitable alternative. He is alert and delights in competition. Quizzes and the opportunity to grapple with thought problems can be a real challenge to him now.

Verbalized criticism is a byword with him, as he voices his likes and dislikes very adamantly. This, however, is generally balanced with a good sense of humor.

Suggestions: Stimulate his thinking to wider areas and guide his verbal expression. Give him good reasons for doing things and teach him to base his decisions on fact, not emotion. This will assist him to weather some difficult moments.

Present the Scriptures in such a way that he finds the meaning and answers for himself. Also present them in a practical daily-related manner. If the truths are pertinent to his needs, and he sees the value in the Scripture, he will grasp hold and be challenged to a personal Bible study.

Because he is so critical and judgmental, he can be shown a standard by which he can make discernments—and this standard is in the Scriptures. He will, however, still need your help in solving some of his problems, so don't leave him to his own resources too quickly.

Socially

The adolescent is a social creature, becoming more preoccupied with social activities the older he becomes. The younger teen likes team activities, but the ninth grader is more interested in social contacts and parties, and resents the younger teenagers. Even with the interest in social contacts, there are many adjustments to make at this time and the problems that arise seem to dominate his entire life, affecting everything he does! Studies in school may falter during this period as this other interest has precedence.

Both boys and girls now have more interest in one another with increased numbers dating and "going steady." Girls mature ahead of boys and become interested in the opposite sex about a year sooner. They sometimes give the appearance of being more aggressive in their social contacts and prefer to date older boys.

Group activities are very popular now, for the junior higher feels less conspicuous and more comfortable in social situations. Clowning around and showing off is a very normal activity for him.

He has a strong desire to be treated as an adult and not a child. Adult restraints are cast aside—or at least he attempts to cast them aside. The desire to be an individual is strong and any type of control by adults or those in authority may be resisted or resented.

Suggestions: Group activities are essential now and some young people will have to be taught how to act within a group. Mixer games or activities that enable campers to get to know one another right away help create a healthier social atmosphere.

In his group Bible study the junior high camper likes to discuss his own doubts, feelings and thoughts. These discussions are very popular and helpful, if handled correctly. He needs an atmosphere that doesn't draw too much attention to him. Show him how Christ will help him grow up and how God cares for any and all problems by pointing out the guidelines for behavior found in Scripture. The teachings of Paul in the Epistles can be very applicable here. If the campers can live according to the teachings while at camp and experience the satisfaction of achieving better relations, then you have been a successful counselor.

This is the opportunity to challenge him to use his social contacts and involvement for witnessing. This can begin while at camp with some of the non-Christian youth and can carry over when he returns to his community.

Don't be surprised if you get a negative reaction at your first meeting. You represent authority to the junior higher. In time, by being friendly and fair, good rapport can be established. He needs someone to confide in and you are the most likely candidate. Your guidance and lack of bossiness when dealing with him will pay rich dividends. By opening up to you and admiring you, the junior high camper gives you the opportunity to present Jesus Christ and the Christian life.

Now that he is seeking independence, assist him in seeing that when one becomes independent, one also assumes more responsibilities. The responsible person is one who shows that he is capable of growing up and deserves independence. Some rules are necessary and most of them are for our own protection and security. Point out that the guidelines and pattern for living found in Scripture enable him to really live life and get the most from it. If he sees these principles in action in your life, and finds that they really work, then he will follow you and grasp the Scriptures as his guide.

Emotionally

This is a trying time and one of upheaval. Frustration, new and uncontrolled emotions, impulsiveness, uncertainty—all these characterize the young adolescent. Don't attempt to predict what he will do or say; this is involved in his thrust for independence. He finds it difficult to make the transition from childhood to adolescence and he lacks confidence. He can't be sure of himself, nor the reactions of others to him. Acceptance is very important, particularly with his own peer group. The opinion of adults does count, too. But because of his uncertainty, he is sometimes willing to try just about anything. Much of this is due to the fact that he really doesn't know what he wants. His imagination can be vivid and his outward emotions or reactions may be the opposite of what he's really feeling, shielding his true feelings.

Suggestions: Patience, understanding and love will heal many of the torments he experiences. If you expect adult or older adolescent behavior from him, you'll be disappointed. Respect him for what he is and work with him. Help him feel wanted and respected. Help him to set some standards for himself and assist him in living up to them. Goals can be set now that will add stability to his life.

Your interest and concern will mean much to him and will pave the way for the presentation of God's love, acceptance and provision. Then he will find that in Christ, he is a new creature. If he can put Christ first in his life, the other things will be put in their proper place. He's looking for a way of life that is acceptable and you can point him to the Christian life. Always stay with a newborn Christian. The Christian life just doesn't happen, but must be nurtured, cultivated and weeded before you can expect to see indications of a harvest. This junior high camper needs you to teach him the way of the Lord.

Spiritually

This can be a time of spiritual awakening as well as a time of doubts. All questions should be dealt with honestly and scripturally. Let him ask his questions and answer them. His spiritual development will depend upon his church background, Bible knowledge and comprehension. This is another age when many make decisions for Christ, but the appeal must not be made on the basis of emotion. All Bible study must be relevant and directed toward his needs.

He can derive satisfaction from the Scriptures and from a time of personal study. Some of the newer Bible versions can make this a much more meaningful experience, and it's the wise counselor who goes prepared. Prayer will be very personal and self-directed at this time, but he can learn to be concerned for friends at camp, non-Christian friends at home, family, his home church, missionaries and the camp. As he hears your concern and love reflected in your prayers for and with him, he will sense the meaningful richness of a sincere prayer life. His life will be different!

The Senior High Camper
(Ages 15-17)

Physically

For most high school campers, this is the time of reaching physical maturity. As you watch this group consume food, you get the impression that they have been starved for weeks before descending upon your campgrounds. They abound in energy. Their coordination is being refined. They are also sexually mature.

Suggestions: Camp activities should include a well-balanced athletic program, suited to the needs of both girls and fellows and allowing for plenty of opportunity to get the necessary exercise. The high schooler needs to be encouraged to get proper rest and take good care of his body. Remind him that his body is the temple of the Holy Spirit. You may need to give health instructions and discussions concerning the use of tobacco, drugs and alcohol. These topics are usually part of the discussion periods. Some high school students are already involved in their usage and others are wondering about them. The facts you present must be valid and current, but the scriptural approach pointing out God's guidelines for one's life is your final authority.

Mentally

The high school student is sharp! Reasons are a must when you ask him to do or believe anything. He questions constantly and is peaking in his ability to learn. He thinks logically, he investigates, evaluates and wants to make his own decisions. Arguments are common as he likes to think that he has the last word and is right. Because he is so close to adulthood, the drive for independence is very evident and the sense of being capable of handling his own affairs is prominent. Vocational interest is one of his major concerns as parents and teachers are pressing him for a decision in order to guide and direct his future schooling. Imagination is vivid but he is concerned with reality.

Suggestions: Mental challenges are needed by this age group and a camp program emphasizing physical exercise and lacking in mental stimulation will create biblical illiterates. Let the young person express his views and questions, but study Scripture so you have at least some of the answers he will ask for. His mentality, as well as his vocational future, needs to come under the direction of God. His mental capabilities can be used for God and he is capable of serious Bible study. Books and Bible study programs can be of great service to him when he returns to his home. He will listen to you more if you respect and accept the fact that he is more independent and is moving closer to adulthood. Asking for his opinion, assistance and guidance, in place of bossing, will help to gain his acceptance. Show him that God has a plan for his life and has set standards and rules for living which must be obeyed. Don't hesitate to challenge him with thought-provoking questions during your cabin devotions, but know when to remain quiet, listening as he speaks and answers his own questions. Pray *with* him, as well as *for* him, and perhaps you will be able to show him how his prayers have been answered—even during the week of camp.

Socially

The high school camper is socially gregarious. This is often one of the most important areas of his life and he must be accepted by the right people, club and clique or his world crumbles. Often he sacrifices his own values in order to be accepted. He cannot tolerate feeling left out. He probably has his own close group of associates. Parties are important outlets, fashions must be the latest and amusements providing thrills and action are part of the high school years. Going steady is very common and provides security. The area of sex poses many problems and most high school students have conflicts over the extent of their sexual behavior. Even those with strong moral standards have difficulty controlling this impulse. Boy-girl relationships sometimes dominate every area of his life, including his involvement in church activities.

Suggestions: Help him feel accepted within the cabin and the entire camp community. Cliques should be avoided and campers should be encouraged to widen their social contacts. Attempt to draw those who are shy into social activities and cabin discussions. It is very easy to respond favorably to the bright, outgoing and socially aggressive person while ignoring the quiet, perhaps inhibited person, but the latter may need you more than the other. No matter what the case, don't favor any individual or group. The quiet one needs greater discrimination in the field of friendships and needs to develop judgment with reference to people. Help him to know that God accepts him completely—no matter what. When we respond to God's invitation, He responds even more greatly to us. All individuals can become something through Jesus Christ.

If you can suggest activities and opportunities that will develop self-confidence in social situations, the high schooler's total life adjustment will be more acceptable to him and to others. Counseling on boy- and girlfriend problems will consume a large portion of your time. Your own standards and patterns must be well established before you can guide in this area. You might let him know that you and the speakers are available for counseling on any area, including this one. Good Christian books can be presented and used while at camp and your camp discussions may have a tendency to center around this topic. Be careful, however, that all of your cabin devotions and discussion times aren't dominated by this topic even though it is a favorite. The Scripture has a frank and thorough presentation about sex and its role in our lives. Delve into the Scriptures and direct him to God's standard. Show how God can help him to govern his body.

Emotionally

Emotions are still intense and fluctuating, but the high schooler is beginning to be more stable and dependable. He is sensitive and may attempt to conceal his feelings. His needs range from security to thrills and he is aware of how he appears and feels. He is planning for the future, but the future offers some uncertainty to him. He must consider marriage, college, work or the military.

Suggestions: This is the time when he needs to consider and appreciate others, as well as himself, and attempt to meet the needs of those about him. By realizing his importance to God, he can feel secure and accepted. He may need encouragement and assistance in considering what to do in the future. Perhaps you can help him choose a school. If you lack experience and knowledge, guide him to someone who can help him. Now he can be challenged to life service in the area of Christian vocations. Work with him to discover God's will for his life through commitment, prayer and Bible study. Assist him in finding healthy expressions and acceptable ways of expressing his emotions.

Spiritually

This can be a time of spiritual conflicts and doubts, but it can also be a time when there is a warm, personal faith. It is a period when many drop away from their church because of the influence of friends, the lack of a well-developed faith or, even more unfortunate, a failure of the church to reach them. Think through with the young person the great and important doctrines of the Christian faith. Dogmatism is disliked in others, but he will appreciate and accept the authority of the Scriptures if you honestly deal

SUMMARY CHART OF CAMPER CHARACTERISTICS

	Juniors (9-11)	Junior Highers (12-14)	Senior Highers (15-17)
Physically	Craves constant activity Likes to wrestle, run, hike, climb, etc. Strong and healthy Girls taller than boys Loves adventure activities Enjoys competition Restless and wiggly Unquenchable curiosity	Rapid, uneven growth spurts Voice change expected May appear awkward Girls are more developed Rapid response to action Pubertal growth evident Preoccupation with looks Self-image tied to looks Allergies are common	Reaching growth maturity Healthy appetite! Coordination refined Sexual maturity Nervously overactive Susceptible to the common cold Girls increase in weight and strength
Mentally	Relational thinkers Use concrete examples only Endless questions: Why? How? When? Where? Keen ability to memorize Loves real life stories	Has reasoning ability Likes fantasy, imagery Investigative Critical, negative spirit Good sense of humor Easily distracted May ignore adult help	Can think in abstracts Reasoning ability sharp Thinks logically, soundly Wants full independence Arguments are common Vocational interest high Imagination is vivid

	Juniors (9-11)	Junior Highers (12-14)	Senior Highers (15-17)
Mentally (Con't)	Attention span: 20-40 minutes Creativity at a peak now Learning activities are a must	Still eager to memorize Snap judgments	Concerned with reality Social consciousness
Socially	Accepts limited responsibility Respects authority Favors peers from same sex Favors friends the same age Some interest in dating Teamwork is important Wants group acceptance "Best friends" change often Can be bossy and demanding	Enjoys group activities Resents younger teenagers Interest in opposite sex Aggressive in society Interest in school drops Problems dominate life Daring, defiant, difficult "Anti" attitude Needs love, understanding	Quite gregarious This is a high priority Peer acceptance essential Going steady is common Conflict w/sexual values Spends a lot of time with friends Moral standards unsure Search for identity Thrill-seeking attitude

Emotionally	Quick tempered Dislike outward affection Good sense of humor Displays a value system Little control over emotions Desires some independence Mood swings evident Fear of failure Peer pressure formation	Emotions fluctuate Feels misunderstood Severe mood swings common Very unpredictable Thrust for independence Hides true feelings Requires great patience Needs acceptance as he is May devaluate parents	Emotions still fluctuate Still may be intense May be withdrawn Envious of success Materialistic Wants responsibilities Tests authority models
Spiritually	Can't grasp abstracts Can't grasp symbolism Use object lessons with care Avoid emotional appeals Questions spiritual issues Salvation decision possible Simple trusting faith Can have quiet times Hero worship strong Needs good role models	Spiritual awakening Relate Bible to needs Self-directed prayer Childhood beliefs lost May doubt God's love Readiness to accept Christ Can't cope with past failures Can have quiet times Questions biblical values Needs strong role models	Conflicts and doubts Accepts abstracts Wavering faith Heavily peer influenced Dogmatism is disliked Enjoys testimonies May appear indifferent but is still listening His faith is personal

with his doubts. The faith of another Christian can have a stabilizing influence on him so the personal testimonies of other Christians he admires will carry a lot of weight. The high school camper needs to have an active and expressive faith; use him at camp. Motivate and utilize him in Christian service or he may be lost to the Church. He may look forward to counseling someday as a number of camps use older high school students as counselor trainees or junior counselors.

Questions for Further Discussion

1. As you reflect back on the three different age group characteristics, which group would be the most and least enjoyable for you to work with?
2. What camper behavior(s) will be the most difficult for you to overlook? Why?
3. What camper behavior will be the hardest for you to deal with at camp?
4. How will you respond when that behavior is demonstrated by one of your campers?
5. What Bible stories from the Old and New Testaments will you be able to share with junior campers?
6. What will you say to your camper if you discover that they are becoming too affectionate with a member of the opposite sex?
7. How will your methods of disciplining campers differ from a junior to a junior high camper? From a junior high to a senior high camper?
8. Why is it so important to discipline a camper in private?
9. Why is it so important for junior campers to take an afternoon nap and get to bed at an early hour? What can you expect to see in their attitude and behavior if they don't?

5
Disciplining the Camper

There will be times when you must discipline your campers. Since they are away from their parents it is important that you become their guardian. Sometimes it will be difficult to walk the fine line between being a friend and a parent. You will, at moments, have to watch over them to be sure they are not misbehaving, hurting other campers or damaging camp property. Some camp counselors find it difficult to assume this role but it is essential for an effective counselor. And if you are unable to discipline your campers, they will have little respect for you as a counselor and won't follow instructions. Chaos will be the likely result.

The manner with which you discipline your campers can be seen in your style of leadership. For this reason it is important to understand your leadership style *before* you learn methodologies of camper discipline. As you read through the following section, try and see which of these styles best represents your approach.

Common Leadership Styles

Place: The craft hut at a Christian camp located high in a mountain range.

Time: Afternoon during free time.

Situation: Nine-year-old Jimmy is struggling to construct an object with hammer, glue and nails. He hopes to finish the project by the time camp is over so he can take it home and give it to his parents. Hopefully, it is going to be a small bookcase with a Scripture verse burned into each side. He is having difficulty, though, as he is trying to nail the pieces together with nails that are too weak; they are bending and not holding the wood together. You are the counselor. How would you attempt to help him?

Authoritative Leadership

If your concept of leadership is the authoritarian type, you'll jump right in and say, "Here, I'll do that for you. You're doing it all wrong. Watch me. You can't glue it that way and you can't use nails that bend!" Whether an individual is involved in a craft project or a group is participating in a service project, this method operates on basically the same premise: the authoritative leader dictates all policies, techniques *and* activities. In work situations, only one step is mentioned at a time and members are uncertain of the next step.

This "leader" leads primarily by force and causes fear in his followers. He generally has an inflated view of himself so he doesn't consider the opinions or suggestions of others. Some of his methods stem from personal insecurity. No questioning of his authority or plans is encouraged or permitted, and disobedience to the established rule usually brings certain punishment.

For the most part authoritative leaders have difficulty controlling their tempers and they sometimes delight in bossing others. When work tasks are assigned, such as cleaning up the cabin or the campgrounds, these leaders pick who does what and with whom. Praise or criticism is meted out in a personal manner, but for the most part authoritarians remain aloof from the rest of the group. Obedience and productivity are stressed but basic respect and acceptance of individual importance is lacking. The authoritarian method accomplishes much as far as time is concerned, but it also creates varied reactions. Hostility, aggression and fear are very common. Some campers respond with complete and unhesitant obedience, whereas others begin to detest all types of authority and discipline.

Laissez-faire Leadership

Let's return to Jimmy, who is having difficulty with the weak nails and his bookcase. If you believe in laissez-faire leadership, how will you approach this situation? Well, you will act completely opposite of the authoritarian. You will give barely any help to our young, struggling (and by this time, frustrated) camper. You will sit by, observe and leave him to figure it out for himself. You favor almost complete freedom for a group or individual, with an absolute minimum of leader participation.

The laissez-faire leader makes it very clear that he will participate at the minimum level or not at all. He feels that a group or an individual can develop self-reliance and have positive learning experiences by practicing complete self-direction. He goes along with what the group suggests. The difficulty here is that many campers aren't ready for this loosely structured situation. They are disorganized because of the lack of leadership. This approach presumes considerable strength and ability on the part of the group. Campers don't respect the lack of discipline on the part of the leader and would prefer to have limits and some guidance. Very little work is accomplished with this approach.

Democratic Leadership

Let's return for the last time to the craft hut where Jimmy is being approached by you, the democratic counselor. As you approach, you perceive what has happened and comment, "It looks like that's going to be pretty wobbly. Do you have any idea why?" Jimmy thinks a minute and replies, "Well, I've been putting in all these nails but most of them bend and this thing wiggles all over. It looks like only two or three have gone through. Would these thicker nails work better?" You reply, "That just might do the trick. Why not try them and if you like I'll hold the wood so it's steady." This is the democratic approach as it applies to the individual.

When democracy is applied to the group, it means that all policies and decisions are a matter of total group involvement. The group discusses and decides; you encourage and assist. You really enjoy your campers, knowing when to have a good time with them and when to exercise control.

In a way, the democratic process is slower than authoritarian leadership, as you need more time to discuss and plan. But it also means total involvement of the individuals of your group or cabin unit. *You realize that it's better from your perspective to wait and let the group decide than to jump in and accomplish the task— probably in a more efficient and quicker manner, too. You help the group learn how to make decisions. There is free expression of opinions and feelings and individual differences are utilized.* This approach usually results in satisfying interpersonal relations among the campers and counselor. Productivity is not always as high under this type of leadership. However, you evaluate the needs of the situation and help the group to the greatest possible extent within any limitations the group may have.

Democratic leadership, as well as other methods, should be evaluated, as there are some weaknesses. Don't leave the group so alone that they are unable to operate and deteriorate into the laissez-faire method. Each group will react in a different manner—depending upon its constellation—so be ready to adjust. And don't expect the next group to be like the last one. If the campers haven't had training in the democratic process, don't expect them to quickly assume this type of decision making. You'll have to spend time training them. On the other hand, don't become discouraged with a new group and assume that they are incapable of learning or will be unresponsive.

Are you asking, "Which method should I use?" or "Should I use all three?" Most camps favor the democratic method with the realization that it isn't always used in its purest form. Certain rules are fixed and have to be maintained. Your camp will probably suggest guidelines for you to use in your leadership. Some have attempted to alternate from one to another, depending upon the situation. However, this changeable approach can lead to confusion and frustration on the part of the group. The democratic method (with variations, if necessary) has proved to be the best method of leadership.

Qualities of an Effective Leader

An effective leader makes use of his own natural ability. You may not have a thorough knowledge of leadership techniques, but if you're willing to learn and improve, you are on the right track. The following list presents the ideal leader. While no one expects you to exhibit all of these qualities of leadership, it should be your goal to incorporate as many of these qualities as possible into your role as leader.

These qualities are:

1. He leads by example.
2. He has a good sense of humor and exercises it to avert crises and keep molehills from becoming mountains.
3. His thoughts are not inverted toward himself, but rather outwardly toward the greater "we."
4. He capitalizes on the power of suggestion and subtly plants ideas to sprout and grow. He leaves the group free to pick up the hint and proceed to enthusiastically carry it out, making it their own, improving and altering it as many minds go to work.
5. He tactfully avoids serious misunderstandings and feuds with others and sincerely attempts to see their side of the question. He realizes that if he once arouses another's antagonism, he has probably lost all chance to influence him in the future.
6. When there is work to be done, he is in the midst of it, sleeves rolled up and hands dirty.
7. He understands the force of group pressure and group opinion. He realizes that there is danger in letting campers entirely rule themselves. They still have immature judgment and can be cruel and go to extremes when judging each other.
8. He is mindful of the value of "fun," for happy campers seldom become problems. If he is teaching a new skill, he is thorough, but patient and understanding, and proceeds with an infor-

mal, friendly manner. He knows the value of a laugh and always has time for a good joke. He devises ways to make chores fun instead of irksome tasks.

9. He knows that campers, no matter how much they complain and grouse, do not really enjoy slovenly, careless standards of conduct. They soon lose respect for a leader who tolerates such laxness. He recognizes that a request gets better response than an order but that, when orders have been found necessary, they must be enforced.

10. He gives praise freely and can see good in nearly everything and everybody. He realizes that insincere or overused praise is quickly detected and discounted. He avoids nagging and excessive fussiness about detail.

11. He foresees an impending crisis and tries to avert it if he can. If Johnny is chanting how much he dislikes spinach, he does not wait until the whole table is lamenting their pet dislikes, but quietly introduces a new topic. A good leader anticipates situations and makes adequate preparations for them.

12. He shuns public scenes whenever possible. A "bawling out" before others hurts a camper's pride and makes him react by (1) giving up, or (2) growing resentful and intent on revenge. *The effective leader knows that emotional hurts are even more serious than physical ones. He gives the erring camper a chance to "save face" by seemingly ignoring his misdemeanor in public but later takes it up with him privately in a frank and friendly manner.* He knows that "badness" often results from embarrassment or not knowing just what is the right thing to do. *He rejects bad conduct but not the camper guilty of it.*

13. He seldom tells a camper what to do, but instead discusses the problem with him, drawing out the correct solution from him. He never sends a camper away dejected and hopeless but leaves him realizing that the counselor still has faith in him. He knows that teaching is accomplished by guidance and not bossiness. All groups and individuals make mistakes and learn from them.

14. He never uses physical punishment. It seldom brings about the desired result, is usually against camp rules, and might involve him or the camp in legal difficulties.

15. *He uses disciplinary measures sparingly.* He must be convinced that they are in the best interests of the culprit and that he is not acting vindictively or in an effort to save his own pride. Punishment is so easy to administer and gets such quick and sure results (outwardly, at least) that it is often misused or overused. The superior counselor handles his group so skillfully that serious disciplinary problems seldom occur. However, sometimes the day comes when action can no longer be postponed. People are usually good sports about accepting punishment which is deserved and not based upon partiality and/or spite. When discipline is necessary, it should follow as closely as possible on the heels of the misdemeanor and should bear some relationship to it if possible. For instance, depriving a camper of his dessert would be appropriate only for a dining room misdeed. Using work as a punitive measure belittles it and drags it down from the place of honor it ought to hold. However, it may be appropriate for a camper who has cluttered up the grounds, thrown food around the dining room, or otherwise created extra work for someone else.

16. He knows that people usually live up to what is expected of them and that the best way to get a camper to climb to new heights is to show that he expects him to do just that. Issuing a challenge is a very potent force. If there is a lack of leadership at a particular moment, he senses this and fills the gap and does more than his share willingly.

17. He does not take a camper's bad conduct as a personal affront. He realizes that it is more likely to be a reaction from a past experience or an outside worry. A camper's rebellion at even a reasonable amount of discipline may be caused by having had too much of it at home or school.

18. He satisfies his own basic desires in a healthy way. For instance, he does not secure needed affection by encouraging an unhealthy attachment from a camper. He does not unduly encourage campers to bear tales or slavishly serve him.

19. He seldom bursts forth in momentary anger but instead waits through a "cooling off" period to get the facts and consider all angles so that he can approach it with a cool head and sound judgment.[1]

The Causes of Poor Discipline

When one speaks of motivation and control, the word discipline generally is raised. The word discipline comes from the same Greek word as disciple and, basically, the disciples were learners or pupils. Discipline is a process by which people learn what is acceptable, desirable and pleasant for all.

There are a number of specific behavior problems that can arise and each problem generally has a specific cause. Why do campers behave in such varied ways? Many have unsatisfied needs and in their attempt to satisfy these needs they behave in a socially unacceptable manner. Some are seeking attention or attempting to demonstrate their power. Others have a strong and compelling drive to punish others or get even with them for something. It may be real or imagined. There are also those who feel and act inadequate and they demonstrate their inadequacy. This doesn't mean that the goal or reason is a constant one, for the motivating force behind an action may be different on each occasion.

Do you feel that undisciplined behavior is something the camper willingly seeks to relinquish? Not necessarily, as this behavior can be very satisfying to him. Most individuals give up a satisfaction only for a substitute that is more satisfying. If your discipline is going to be effective, you need to know what the camper's actions do for him, what he receives from them and how satisfying the reward is to him. Determine his unfulfilled needs and attempt to meet them. They may be needs that should have been met many years before and you'll just scratch the surface as you attempt to work with him.

Don't expect too much if you have a serious problem; others may have tried to handle it before you with no success. Discipline is a process and takes thought, perception, time and prayer. If you consider discipline just an emergency measure, the results you achieve won't be permanent. Little, if any, learning will have taken place.

Less Effective Methods of Discipline

Controlling and motivating a group of enthusiastic campers

can present a challenge to even the most experienced counselor and camp worker. There are always several answers to a discipline or motivational problem and these answers may be right or wrong at a given time. The kind of discipline you use will have to be directly related to the specific goal you have in mind. The devices mentioned here are the ones most frequently used. Some are effective and others are quite poor. The poorer ones are presented to show some of the possible results you'll want to avoid.

Just picture yourself settling down in your cabin with your campers all tucked into their bunks and ready to go to sleep. You are unable to get to sleep because one of the fellows is an incessant talker and refuses to settle down and be quiet. He whispers, laughs and throws candy at the campers at the other end of the cabin. How will you solve this? How will you deal with him? Here are some disciplines that have been tried:

"Because I Said So" Technique

This is done by going to the boy and stating, "I simply won't have my sleep and the sleep of the other campers disturbed by your messing around. I just won't tolerate this!" What you've done here is to make yourself the object against which his misbehavior is now directed. If he has a desire to please you, he'll be quiet, but if he wants to react to you and keep you riled, he'll continue his actions. This has now become a personal involvement between two individuals, a power struggle between you. Before, it was simply a matter of not settling down and going to sleep. Don't use yourself as the final authority or indicate that this is going to be a struggle between the camper and you.

"Think About It This Way" Approach

Here we have the same situation, but approach it differently by saying: "Well, it looks like you really aren't sleepy yet. What do you think the results might be if you don't get your sleep tonight and you keep the others awake?" This is putting the responsibility back on the camper and assisting him in coming up with the proper solution. You may have to rephrase the question and ask it several times before he'll settle down enough to give you a serious answer. But when he does, you'll have the opportunity to agree and reinforce his solutions or reinterpret them for him.

Helping campers to sense and predict the logical consequences of an act can develop into an applicable learning experience about life. Sometimes individuals have to experience the natural consequences of an action before the lesson is fully learned. Natural consequences represent the pressure of real life. This may be all right as long as there is no injury to people or damage to camp property. You may, for example, have a camper who can never be on time for the daily horseback riding. You tell him that he'll miss his ride if he is late, but you always hold up everyone else until this boy comes trooping down to the stable. If he experiencd the logical consequence of missing a ride one day he might not be late the next time!

Research and practical study indicates that letting children and teenagers experience the natural consequences of their misbehavior is a very important factor in maintaining order. Correct behavior and adherence to rules arise from within when this method is implemented. A child soon realizes that it is more satisfying to respect rules and regulations than to break them.

This method does not demand any submission to another person, either! However, all too often counselors either become too impatient with this method or move out of pity, giving in and thus breaking down everything that they have worked toward. You are teaching respect for order and rules and are helping to develop healthy conformity. The camper is better off experiencing the natural consequences of his action rather than the punishment administered by someone other than himself. Consequences are a natural result of breaking the rules so place the responsibility for changing the situation on the camper.

The "Think About It This Way" approach will break down if the tone of your voice implies punishment. Instead, place the responsibility on the camper, as one camp director did. The camp insisted on timeliness and all campers had to be in the dining hall on time. Anyone arriving more than 10 minutes late would have to miss that meal. Several campers developed the habit of coming in consistently eight or nine minutes late and it wasn't long before their calculations were off and they arrived at the dining hall too late. One of the counselors wanted to let them go ahead and eat. He felt it would be cruel to make them go hungry for the afternoon. The camp director, however, handled the situation in a way that produced results. He approached the campers and mentioned that he was sorry they had arrived too late. But the rules of camp had been explained to everyone and anyone arriving late would have to miss the meal. Since they had chosen to be late, they had also made the choice of missing the meal. If they would like to eat the next meal, they would certainly be welcome to do so if they were there on time. You can imagine the results. When dinnertime rolled around the first in line were the hungry fellows and from then on they were there on time. It was left up to the campers to change the situation.

"I Only Like the Good Kids" Threat

This is often used by the improperly trained counselor and is most ineffective. This counselor, when approaching the sleepless camper problem, says either, "Now look, it's late and we want to get our sleep. I really like kids who are quiet and conform to the rules. Now if you want me to like you, BE QUIET!" or, "If you continue to disturb us, you might as well forget me as your friend. I don't care for campers who don't follow orders." Neither of these threats are very convincing or effective.

"That's Very Good" Opening

People respond quite favorably to praise and compliments when they are used honestly and in proper proportion with other comments. Some campers can become dependent upon your words of praise, however, because they never experience commendation in their homes. Their day can be made or broken by the amount of praise that you give. People who are praised are usually inclined to continue the behavior that won recognition. Be certain this is not flattery or verbal bribery, for it will be obvious if it is.

"Do It or Else" Method

When tempers begin to rise and everything else you have

tried seems to fail, it is a temptation to gain control by making threats. But threats usually bring only momentary results. The most frequent types of threats appeal to *morals*—"Nice boys or girls never do anything like that"; *age status*—"Hey there, you're not 10 years old, you're 14, so why not act like it?" or "Big kids don't do that sort of thing around this camp"; *sex status*—"Don't be a sissy, all the other fellows took an early morning dip. Aren't you a man yet?"; *parental control*—"Say, if you can't learn to conform, I'm just going to have to write your folks and we'll see what they have to say about this kind of thing"; or *higher authority*—"Do it just one more time and I'm taking you to the girl's dean and then you'll really get it."

The use of any kind of higher authority in the camp can be functional if used in a non-threatening manner. But only as a last resort should you go to the camp director with a behavior problem—and be careful not to make the camp dean or director a boogie man. All camps have some basic rules and standards and this can be the final source of authority, instead of blaming a person. The director or dean can aid in enforcing these rules, but to use them as a threat is unfair to *them*. You may limit their effectiveness in doing personal work with the campers by prejudicing the campers. Never use a threat which you don't intend to carry out.

Appealing to group status by asking, "How do you think the others are going to feel about you if you continue to act like this?" has proven effective *if* used and presented in a way that will be acceptable to the problem camper. The inflection of your voice is so very important as you attempt to motivate and guide others. It might not be *what* you say but the *way* you say it that determines the outcome.

Methods which should not be used include ridiculing, sarcasm, shaming, bribing, causing fear or ignoring the person. Now and then, these may seem to solve the problem for the moment, but what other and more serious problems are they helping to create? Misunderstood discipline or cruelty in any physical or mental form should not be used.

Many of the suggestions mentioned so far are the type that camps prefer to have left at home. They have no place in proper leadership and motivation, but there are some that can be extremely effective.

Effective Disciplinary Methods

1. Ask for individual or group evaluation. "What do YOU think of that?" Show that you're interested in his opinion and enlist his cooperation in what is important at that particular moment. Sometimes it helps to talk over the rules, getting his reactions on what to do when there is a rule infraction. You can also use your skill to make the group members more secure. This will promote better group discipline through cooperative action.

2. Put the choice in the camper's hands with acceptance of the consequences. "Well Jim, it seems like you've got a choice here. You can either follow the rules, like the rest of the guys, and stay here at the pool *or* you can keep breaking the rules and give up swimming for a couple of days. *You* make the choice." This has proven to be a very effective method as the camper realizes that he is directly responsible for his behavior and his reaction to it. He can't blame anyone but himself if restrictions have been imposed because the rules were broken.

3. Show enthusiasm. "Hey, let's go for it. It looks like fun."

4. Offer suggestions and explanations. "Why not try it *this* way?"

5. Pose a problem. Even though you may have the answer, let him have the fun of thinking it through. At the same time you'll capture his attention and direction.

6. Point out alternatives. "We could approach this in several ways. Why not try this first?"

7. Ask the group to look at itself to see progress. "How are we doing?"

8. Suggest resources. "Maybe the craft director could give us a hand here."

9. Take pride in the group. This develops group unity, spirit and allegiance to you, your suggestions and your requests. Instead of orders use "we" and "let's," not "I." If the camper likes you and respects you as a counselor, you won't need to

motivate. If you want him to be disciplined, he must see a disciplined leader. He'll follow! Varying activities and keeping him busy will achieve wonders.

10. Solicit group consensus. This method allows the campers to set their own rules inside their cabin, i.e. making their beds each morning, picking up wet towels, etc. After the campers have decided on some basic rules allow them to make up the penalties for breaking them. For example, if a camper doesn't make his bed in time for inspection he must make all of the other campers' beds the next morning. Be sure you don't let the penalties get out of hand. They should suit the offense and be within reason.

Remember, discipline is worthless unless it does more than just stop poor behavior. Effective discipline is directed toward the underlying sources of the difficulty, not toward the symptoms. It looks toward the future and is not so concerned with the past.

If you are angry, wait and collect your wits and your feelings before you proceed. Be sure you are right, then proceed with fairness. Firmness is not measured by loudness. Avoid false accusations and don't jump to conclusions. Commands should be minimal and don't be a picky counselor; be concerned with major not minor issues. If you make a mistake be able to laugh at yourself and apologize.

As you approach a loaded situation and a crisis is impending, proceed with caution. Kids often think it is fun to get a counselor riled up. Are you certain you have established discipline or is there just temporary conformity? There IS a difference.

Questions for Further Discussion

1. Of the three leadership styles that were presented, which one most clearly represents your style?
2. If your style is not that of the democratic leader, how will you be able to adjust your present style?

3. Why is the democratic style the most effective for a camp counselor to possess?

4. Which effective leadership qualities do you presently possess? Which ones are your strongest?

5. Of those qualities, which ones do you not possess at this time? What will you do between now and the beginning of camp to appropriate them?

6. Review the less effective methods of discipline. Which one would you most likely use? How will you avoid using that technique at camp?

7. Review the effective methods of discipline. Which ones will you try and use as a camp counselor?

8. What type of poor behavior will be the hardest for you to deal with as a camp counselor? What will you do when that behavior is demonstrated by one of your campers?

9. What will you do when you feel yourself beginning to lose control or getting to the "end of your rope"?

10. Who can you go and talk to when you have exhausted all of your attempts to discipline a camper?

6
Counseling the Camper

Counseling is a relationship in which one person tries to help another to understand and solve problems. It is an understanding between persons which results in a change. It sometimes involves advice-giving, information-giving, interpretation of situations and encouraging the other person to think out or work out his difficulties. Often it involves just listening. Basically, it is a communication process; he speaks to you and you respond to him.

Christian counseling is unique because in the final analysis your counseling will lead to Christ. Your final source of authority is the Scripture. It supplies the answer for every problem in the person of Jesus Christ and offers an authoritative guide for conduct in the Word of God. Therefore, your counseling has a deeper function—that of training a girl or boy to relate every aspect of life to Christ and look to Him each moment.

Keys to Effective Communication

There are many practical considerations. Camping may be an entirely new situation for a camper. You may not know him and he doesn't know you. The better you become acquainted, the more opportunities will be presented for you to counsel with him. You may have 10 campers but don't think of them as just a group of boys or a group of girls—each is an individual and you need to think of him as such. Learning his name the very first day will make your job that much easier.

You may have some who will reject you. No matter how hard you try, there won't seem to be any breakthrough. Don't try to force yourself on any camper—all people are different. One camper may open up to you the first day. Another may wait until an hour before he leaves camp. People respond at different times and for different reasons.

The home backgrounds and environments from which campers come vary tremendously. Many come from homes in which there is division, separation and divorce. Some may not have a father or mother at home. During the camp, you may be filling that need. Others will come from homes in which the family is entrenched in the church program and the children may fit well into camp. Or, they may be very rebellious. Be sympathetic toward all, no matter what the backgrounds. Try to understand each camper in light of his environmental background and present status.

Don't assume at the beginning of the camp that you have some campers who have no difficulties at all. Some may not, but you have to know them well before this assumption can be made. Quite often the quiet model child has more problems than the boisterous ones in your dorm. All behavior has significance.

As you show that you have a personal concern for each one and attempt to get close to him, openings will present themselves. Without prying, learn everything you can about each camper—age, interests, hobbies, position in family, social status, church background, camping experience, etc. To be a counselor, you have to be perceptive enough to realize when something is going on in the life of a child or adolescent. Often, just one word at the right time is all that is necessary to provide the opportunity to help.

Be sensitive to the camper who may be trying to establish a contact with you. It could be someone in your own cabin or in someone else's group. If you notice that someone seems to hang back after a meeting or stays to help you do something in the dorm, this may be the time. Occasionally, he will begin with a question and ask your opinion. In doing this, he may be testing you to see if you're an accepting type of person and if you'll be willing to listen to any problem. Some have been known to begin by saying, "Hey, I've got this friend of mine back home and the other day, he and his dad got into a fight over how much money he was spending on himself. He thinks that his kid should help on the expenses of the car. What do you think about this? What should I tell my buddy?" Later, as you talk with him, you may find out that he is this so-called friend! He was hesitant to mention this at the beginning as he didn't know what type of reception he would receive.

Your availability will be an important factor in any counseling you will do at camp. If the campers find you ready and willing to listen, they will seek you out. Don't appear so busy, rushed or important that they feel they are bothering you. You are there at camp to work with them and don't let anything else interfere with your time. If a counseling opportunity arises, "after swimming" or "after lunch" may be too late and the opportunity may be gone.

When people talk to you, do you listen? Can you determine what they are really saying and do you appear interested? Do you wait to hear all of their story before you give your advice? If so, you're doing the right thing. Many times, through the process of "talking it out," a person will be able to find the solution himself without your actually giving advice. This happens if you're a good listener! In order for campers to fully express themselves, they must have your undivided attention. Know when to remain silent. Many a person has curtailed a camper's desire to talk by talking too soon and too much.

Are you able to talk with them on their own level? If so, there will be communication and it will be two-way. Terms and phrases that are ambiguous and foreign to a camper will just confuse the problem. Biblical terms such as "saved" and "born again" and "convicted" may mean a great deal to you, but what does it mean to the young person who lacks a biblical background? When you mention "saved," he might think you're talking about being saved in the swimming pool. "Convicted" might mean guilty of a crime! Use words he will understand and if you use a biblical phrase, explain it to him.

Know up-to-date terms and the current vocabulary of the age group with which you are working. This doesn't mean that you always have to use their slang. You'll feel uncomfortable if the words are not a part of your own vocabulary. A good rule to follow is to use known terms to explain the unknown.

A positive attitude on your part, rather than a dogmatic approach, will help your counseling to be accepted. The only area that you can be dogmatic about is the vital, major area of biblical teaching. There will be various feelings and views represented, depending upon the camp, churches and denominations attending. An argumentative spirit in a counselor is a hindrance. If you present a positive picture of Christianity as evidenced by your daily life, others will want what you have.

How shockproof are you? Do you gasp or turn red when you hear about past exploits? Try not to be amazed and excited when you learn of a camper's past and present deeds. This only helps to reinforce that perhaps what he did was quite an event! Maintain your normal appearance and attempt to help by putting him at ease. One of the better methods of doing this, especially if the individual is deeply concerned over the problem, is the fact that many others have faced the same problem and have been able to conquer it.

How do you react to a person who seems to have the answer for everything, even questions and problems out of his realm of knowledge? If your reaction is typical, you usually find out that this type of person isn't worth talking to. He doesn't know as much as he thinks he does. When you don't have the answer to a situation, don't pretend to have one. If you say that you do and the suggestions you give are later found to be invalid, you've destroyed a counseling relationship. You are not a psychologist nor a therapist, but you will still have to cope with problems. Thus, know your abilities and limitations and know when to seek assistance. Be honest and admit that you do have limitations and don't always have the answer. But show that you're willing to try to find the answer or you'll attempt with his permission to help find someone who is able to assist him. Perhaps one of the conference deans or speakers can be of assistance here.

When you are counseling with a child or youth concerning his personal problems, your goal is to find insight and a solution. The insight that you seek in counseling is that which enables a young person to understand his own feelings, attitudes and even motivation. When these are sorted out the reason or basis for his problem will probably become clear.

Quite often, the problems brought to you are the result of faulty attitudes. External behavior is important, but more vital is the feeling or attitude. Jesus was insistent on the necessity of correcting inner attitudes. "But those things which proceed out of the mouth come forth from the heart, and they defile a man. For out of the heart proceed evil thoughts, murders, adulteries, fornications, thefts, false witness, blasphemies" (Matt. 15:18-19, *NKJV*). When inner attitudes are changed or modified, new patterns of behavior come into being. This will come gradually as the two of you work together.

In addition, discovering the consequences of these in one's life will hasten the process of insight. The final phase involves discovering the changes that he can make in his life to alleviate that which has been a hindrance. Often, the changes to be made are within himself, but at times those about him are the cause of the difficulty. It could be parents, siblings, friends, school, church or even the other campers. Then a camper needs to learn how to adjust and work with the situations.

Your final and overall goal in counseling is to lead the camper (when ready) to Jesus Christ and to the rich and full life that knowing Him can provide. You are not just after decisions, but lives that are changed because they have come face to face with Jesus Christ and have accepted Him as Lord, Saviour and Master of their lives.

Basic Counseling Techniques

When you counsel with an individual, be certain you are in a location where you have privacy and he isn't fearful that someone else is listening. Never reveal to other campers what has been told to you in confidence. If this happens, he won't confide in you again. Don't appear anxious or overly concerned as he talks to you. If he is hesitant to express himself, don't start by talking about his problem. Talk about an unemotional subject, one that will put him at ease and allay any fears he has. Try to say those things which will encourage him to continue talking.

What are some practical yet simple techniques that you can use? What do you say? Asking questions can be of great help in aiding a person to verbalize his problems or thoughts. There are several types of questions that can be used.

1. *Information-gaining questions.* There are times when you need to have more facts or perhaps you've forgotten some of the details the person has mentioned. Ask for necessary and specific information about persons, things or occurrences. Sometimes the camper talks as though he thought you understood everything about him when you didn't. Example: "Which sister was that?" "When did you say that happened?"

2. *Clarifying questions.* Often a child or young person is confused about his problems and he conveys this confusion to you as he talks. The clarifying question is important as it may help the camper to become more aware of his own thoughts. It also helps him to present his thoughts in a more logical manner. Example: "Why do you think he didn't like you then?" "How do you think that happened?" "Can you suggest a reason why they did that?"

3. *Reflective questions.* This is the type of a question which reflects back to the camper a portion of what he has said. This is helpful as it enables a person to decide whether what he has just said is really what he means. Camper: "You know, the way the others in this cabin treat me, it's as though I don't even exist. They treat me like dirt sometimes. I wish I'd never come to this camp. I wanted to once, but when you are in a cabin where everyone else hates you, it's no fun." Counselor: "They all hate you?"

4. *Confronting questions.* This type of question should be used sparingly when others haven't been very effective. This question is much more directive and may be used when a camper is unable to recognize what his behavior is doing to him.

This actually helps a person to examine the meaning of his actions. Camper: "Well, I guess I showed that wise guy from cabin four. We haven't been getting along all week and he's been bullying me, but when he ran into that tree during the game, did I ever laugh and rub it in!" Counselor: "You laughed at him? Why was that?" Camper: "Well, it was kind of funny and I wanted to get back at him." Counselor: "How do you think he felt when you laughed at him? Do you think this might keep him from bullying you in the future?"

These are just a sampling of the kind of questions you can use to help your campers. Just as you listen and ask questions, you can also make comments concerning what has been said.

1. *Reflective comments.* Often a camper attempts to sort out his thoughts and feelings, but has difficulty doing so. This is the opportunity for you to assist by restating what he has said, but in somewhat different terminology. For the most part emphasize the intellectual content of what has been said and clarify it. It is most effective in helping the camper clarify the problem. Camper: "The other day, I was surprised when the others in my dorm came up and offered to help me. It really shocked me and I wondered why they did it. They didn't have to and I didn't ask them to. No one else has ever done this. I really wondered why but after awhile, I started thinking that maybe they're trying to put into practice what the speaker has been talking about. Then I wondered if I would have done that." Counselor: "Their helping you surprised you, but perhaps they're putting the teaching into practice and you're not sure if you would do the same or not."

2. *Empathetic comments.* Empathy is very different from sympathy. Sympathy is not always helpful whereas empathy is indispensable for any type of counseling. Sympathy is mostly emotional and often an identification with the person. Empathy is more of an intellectual process in which the counselor attempts to put himself momentarily in the camper's situation without emotional involvement. The word means literally "feeling into," whereas sympathy is "feeling with." Empathy has a much deeper sense of involvement or identification with the other person. It's the thinking or feeling of one person into another so that

some state of identification is achieved. You attempt, in a sense, to be inside the other person and experience the situation from his point of view. Camper: "He really hurt me when he broke up with me after the meeting tonight (crying). He said he didn't care about me any more and didn't want to date me and now he's thinking of going out with my best friend." Counselor: "This is pretty hard on you right now." Camper: "It's about the worst thing that's ever happened to me. It's too much." Counselor: "It's almost more than you can handle right now."

3. *Puzzling comments.* Some campers react in a negative manner when you are direct with them. This type of comment is usually well accepted and can frequently be of great value. When you appear puzzled by what he has said either through your facial expression, attitude or statement, this causes him to clarify what he has said. In turn, this motivates him to rethink or evaluate what he expressed. Phrases on your part can be unfinished, such as "You mean that . . . " or "If I understand you correctly . . . " or "I think I missed what you meant by that."

4. *Confronting comments.* This comment is one that is intended to bring the camper face to face with some phase of his behavior or problem that he hasn't recognized or admitted. This is the type of technique that should be used after some of the less threatening ones have been employed. A camper who is defensive about his behavior and fails to see how he contributes to the problem may have to be confronted directly. Camper: "Boy, I don't know what to do now. The camp dean really let me have it last night. He said my attitude was det—Oh, what was that word? Yeah, detrimental to the whole camp. That's what the guy said. He even had the nerve to say that I griped too much about everything and everybody, and all I wanted to be was a critic. Garbage! I think the dean's all wet! So I do say what I think and some of the things here are pretty crummy. He doesn't have to talk to me like that! I've got my opinion, just like anyone else. He treats me like I was an immature kid, instead of a high school senior. After all, I'll be a college man next year." Counselor: "Do you think that perhaps he feels you act like an immature kid and this is why you deserve to be treated like one?"

5. *Continuation comments.* This is a comment that enables the camper to continue talking. Perhaps he has become frustrated and bogged down and his mind has gone blank. He can't quite succeed in putting his feelings into words and here you can help by making a remark that enables him to continue talking. This increases rapport between the two of you and indicates that you understand what he says and what he means. Camper: "I don't know what's the matter with me. I try so hard to live like a Christian and then blooey—I wreck it all. Just when I think I'm living straight, then I go and blow it. I know what's right and wrong, but I—I just can't seem to keep with it—and—well—I don't know—I—." Counselor: "You know what's right yet you have a difficult time doing it and you can't figure it all out." Camper: "Yeah, that's just about it. I want to do what's right and I know what to do, but then I goof it all up and fall right back into the old pattern. You know? Like the other day I started . . . . "

Other times you may have to *structure a situation.* A camper comes to you and has the desire to talk but doesn't know how to begin or what to expect from you. You may have to suggest to him that he just talk about anything on his mind. Try to work with him to understand his problem and help him come to a solution.

Another method is to use an *understatement* of the problem. A camper is more apt to respond to an understatement than an overstatement.

On other occasions you may have to *redirect the responsibility* for an answer back to the camper if you feel he can make the decision or answer the question himself. He may ask you to answer questions or tell him what to do or say. A response such as, "Well, how do you feel about that?" or "What do you think should be done here?" will thrust the responsibility back to its proper place.

Another time, you may have to convey the feeling that you accept what is being said. This doesn't mean you agree or disagree with what's being expressed but you do understand or are attempting to understand. Example: "Yes." "Hhmm." "I see."

Now and then, you can provide openings or opportunity for discussion by simply saying, "Well, how are things going with you today?" or "You seem to be a little down in the dumps today. What's up?"

Three other types of remarks that you can make are interpretation, approval and reassurance. *Interpretations* are when you point out casual relationships or respond to feelings or ideas that have not as yet been expressed by the camper.

Approval statements are the kind where you evaluate the camper or his ideas in such a way that you provide emotional support.

Reassurance is actually encouraging the person by raising his self-esteem or self-assurance.

In the more directive approach to counseling, you take the responsibility for discovering the nature of the problem and the solution. This method should be reserved for those occasions when the camper is unable to discover the basis of his problem and lacks the necessary insight for a solution. There are occasions when your years of maturity, experience and insight can be of value as you offer suggestions and point out relationships and alternatives. Most novice counselors have the tendency to say, "You should do this" or "This is your problem" or "You should never do it that way." The camper may then begin to tune out your advice. Being directive doesn't allow him to fully express himself nor establish a two-way communication with you. A sparing use of this technique may prove to be the answer with some campers.

These are the counseling techniques so use them wisely and well. Become acquainted with them before you counsel. Remember, your job is to listen, reflect and clarify and not to solve a camper's problems. Help him to gain insight so that he may find the solution to his problem. When insight is developed, you may be able to present Scripture that will deal with the problem involved. Avoid being preachy and let the Scriptures speak to your camper. Caution yourself not to give a personal passage of Scripture or pray with him before he has gained insight into the problem. Prayerfully consider when your camper is ready and receptive for your witness.

Guidelines for Effective Counseling

Consider these recommendations as you counsel:

1. Counseling, to be beneficial, requires a great deal of time. Changes in personality come slowly. Casual advice cannot be construed as counseling.

2. If you do not have highly technical training avoid dealing with difficult cases; rather, you should refer them to an expert in this line. Unskilled counseling may do more harm than good. Recognize the limitations of the layman. Do not use the term "psychoanalyze," and do not attempt psychoanalytic technique.

3. Keep confidences inviolate. If you betray a trust you lose forever your opportunity to be of further help.

4. The best attitude for you to take is that of cheerful, thoughtful objectivity; avoid pronounced sympathizing or condemning. At the same time, of course, show sincere interest and understanding. Learn to be a good listener.

5. Your suggestions may be temporarily useful, but the real solution to a problem can only be discovered by the camper. Instead of trying to impose your will, attempt to help the camper reach his own conclusions and express them in action.

6. The problem as presented may seem to the person in trouble to be insoluble. Even if this were true, he would have to adjust himself to the situation and, therefore, needs help. His problem, however, is probably not unique. Try to see another person in each predicament, and consider how he might solve it.

7. Strange as it may seem, even one who comes voluntarily for help frequently resists your effort to aid him. This resistance may take the form of tardiness, of absence from appointment, of talk about irrelevant matters, and of counterattacks against you or others. This attitude is not necessarily cause for discouragement.

8. Help the camper to discover and understand all of the facts bearing on the case. He may have difficulty in understanding his problem because he does not know or understand all of the facts. At times these facts will be technical and will need interpretation by an expert.

9. Avoid trying to explain his behavior. By use of other cases and by questioning, build up in his mind his own reasonable interpretation. The aim of the talk is to get him to understand his actions.

10. Expect patterns. Great similarity will be found as far as the behavior of individuals is concerned. For instance, many people fear meeting new situations, wish to avoid people, want to run away from a situation, try to project the blame onto someone else, make a mountain out of a molehill.

11. Avoid being maneuvered into emotional behavior. Campers will endeavor to arouse sympathy, to shock you, to hurt you with cutting phrases, to inflate your vanity, to get caresses, to make you pity and care for them, to win rebuke, to provoke outbursts of your own ideas, and so forth. Objectivity takes constant defense.

12. Consider physical condition. Many problems are rooted in bad health. This calls for reliable examination and treatment.

13. Begin at the point where the camper finds difficulty. It may not be the root of the problem, but it is the place where he needs help. It will probably lead to the major problem.

14. So far as possible, where mutual adjustment with other people is involved, work out a solution in the presence of all persons concerned. It is sometimes more necessary to study people who live with the individual than the individual himself.

15. In helping a person to solve his problem, it is seldom possible to depend exclusively upon either bringing about changes in environment or upon the camper securing new insight and attitudes. Both are usually in need of some readjustment.

16. Do not let the channels of exploration be determined by emotional reaction. It is sometimes necessary to say things which hurt the camper. If you are sure the surgery is needed, go ahead calmly.

17. Avoid dependence upon verbal solutions. Test them in action.

18. Don't try to save your own face. In many respects, you may be less well-adjusted than the camper. Grow with him; don't reach down a helping hand from too high up.

19. One easy and frequently helpful step is to remove the camper's fear that he is the only person in the world with his type of difficulty.

20. Avoid focusing on too distant goals without adequate attention to immediate steps. Help the camper to plan steps for improvement now.

21. Even when the simplest words and illustrations have been used, be sure that you will be understood, especially if you are talking about a camper's weaknesses.

22. Watch for building stereotypes. Don't try to classify a certain person or type of behavior without investigation. Intuition may mislead you often if it is not discounted.

23. Occasionally, overhaul your motives in counseling. Give due weight to the vicarious thrill of hearing about misdeeds, the sense of mastery, the delight in secret intimacy, the desire for affection and trust from the young, the enjoyment of a reputation. Try to keep these in proper proportion to the desire for the welfare of the camper.

24. Encourage independence. If the camper continuously depends on you for help, you are unsuccessful. Give only as much help as is absolutely required and reduce this amount constantly. The person who can get along without you is better off than one whom you constantly help.[1]

Leading a Camper to Christ

A camper may seek you out following the Bible study, evening meeting, free time or cabin devotions. Leading a person to Jesus Christ can take place at any time at a camp. Cabin devotions in the evening can be a very rewarding experience. You're alone with just your campers and each one has the opportunity to talk now. You want to know what he is thinking. This is the time to ask and provoke questions. You can lead into this activity by re-emphasizing what the speaker presented that day or by asking questions about what was stated. "What do you like about camp?" and "What have you learned so far?" Later during the camp, questions such as "What do you think a Christian is?" and "What is a Christian like?" will give you an understanding of his comprehension and readiness to make a commitment. The prayer time in the cabin can also be a wonderful experience and can awaken the need within a young person for Jesus Christ.

Your goal in counseling with a camper about Christ is not just a decision but a changed life. Christ assumes the center point in his life. Camps that emphasize the number of decisions sometimes face the problem of creating too much pressure on the campers and end up with some that are superficial. The Holy Spirit must lead in the life of every person to convict him and awaken his need. No commitment should be forced. This is a matter of guidance, not pressure.

The lasting results of a decision made when the individual is mentally and emotionally disturbed are questionable. This was pressed home in a striking and tragic case one time. During a college conference one winter a young man was in attendance who had a multitude of personal problems. He was very impressed with the camp and during the evening communion service appeared very bothered and concerned. After the meeting most of the campers were walking outside in the snow. Suddenly this young man came rushing into the building screaming and crying. He wanted desperately to talk with someone about his problems. A counselor talked with him for over an hour and attempted to assist and counsel him but he remained highly disturbed. Later that evening, he talked with one of the speakers until the wee hours in the morning. He gave all indications of having accepted Jesus Christ as his personal Saviour.

The next evening during a testimony time at his church he gave an extremely dramatic and flowery account of his experience and what he was now going to accomplish. Three weeks later, he was back living the type of life he had been accustomed to and in the coming year, despite efforts to help him, continued in this path. With this boy, the Holy Spirit had not been the motivating factor.

When you are leading a person to Christ, enough time must be taken to be sure that the individual is not distraught and unable to understand what he is doing. How much you will have to explain about salvation will largely depend upon his previous experience and background. Each camper is different and you will have to determine his knowledge and understanding of the Scriptures. Know what he is seeking. The speaker will present the message, will challenge him and give him the opportunity to express his desire for commitment to Christ. Your task is to instruct the camper in his decision for Christ. The Scriptures must be used and reference made to them. Make sure he understands what he is doing and show him that his belief and assurance is founded upon the Scripture.

The more extensive your knowledge and comprehension of the Bible is, the better qualified you will be in using the Scripture. Many basic passages should be known from memory so that you have them at your fingertips. Don't confuse the camper with too many Scriptures. As you work, always use the Bible, even if you know the passage from memory. If possible, have him read the passages aloud. Then you can ask if he understands what he has read.

There are certain basic facts that should be covered from the Scriptures:

1. *The need.* Romans 3:10,23; 6:23.
2. *God's provision for the need.* 1 Peter 2:24; Isaiah 53:5-6; Romans 5:8.
3. *He must do something about the provision of God.* Ephesians 2:8-9; Revelation 3:20; John 1:12.

Another way of presenting the Scripture is this:

1. *The fact of sin.* Romans 3:23.
2. *The penalty of sin.* Romans 6:23.
3. *The penalty must be paid.* Hebrews 9:27.
4. *The penalty was paid by Christ.* Romans 5:8.
5. *Salvation is a free gift.* Ephesians 2:8-9.
6. *He must accept this.* John 1:12.

From a biblical point of view, the camper should be shown how he invites Christ into his life.

1. *It is a matter of personally inviting Jesus Christ into his life.* Revelation 3:20; Romans 10:10.
2. *Jesus Christ has promised that He will come into a person's*

life if he asks, believing. John 6:37.

After the Scriptures have been thoroughly read and explained, have the person pray out loud first and then you pray. Don't pray in place of the camper as this is his time of decision and dedication. You may have to explain to him how to pray and what he can say in his prayer. As you explain prayer to the camper, mention that it is talking to God just as he talks to his friends. God is not interested in big words or solemn tones, but simply wants to hear what is upon his heart. Many will be praying for the first time and the words may come in a hesitant, simple and brief manner. When you follow with your prayer, use simple words and thoughts and don't try to impress the camper with your grasp of theological terms and polysyllabic words.

The camper's prayer should include (a) a recognition that he is a sinner and has done wrong in the sight of God, (b) a realization that Christ died for his sins and (c) an invitation for Christ to come into his life and become Lord and Master. Remember that the prayers and the expressions will vary. If a proper time of explanation and discussion takes place before the prayer, you will be assured that there is understanding, even if his prayer doesn't completely cover everything you've talked about. If the camper's prayer seems inadequate or if it is too brief for you, don't ask him to pray again and cover the areas that he neglected. Prayer is a spontaneous matter and each of us has had to learn how to pray. The fact that he has now prayed and discovered this access to God will be a thrilling experience and one that he will want to repeat daily.

The Follow-Up Program

Well, you say, so that's what is involved and what they mean by counseling. Not exactly; your work has just begun. You've been given the privilege of securing the commitment of the camper but many others were just as involved in this act as you were. Others were praying for this person. The speaker and perhaps the pastor back home laid the groundwork for this decision.

If you ever lead a person to Christ and stop there, you've

failed in your counseling ministry. What is called follow-up or Christian growth must begin immediately and continue during the remainder of the conference. It must also continue when the camper returns to his church. It is tremendously important that you lay a solid foundation on which to build his spiritual life. There is never enough time to work in this realm but in a sense, you will be raising him until he is able to care for himself and in turn go out and spiritually help someone else. If you fail in this task, who will be the one to do it? You are the one in the best position to follow through. Perhaps one of the speakers had the privilege of leading your camper to Christ. You will still be the person involved with his follow-up process.

There are many different methods available for the follow-up program. Because each camper is a distinct personality, it is best to try to fit the material to his need and this necessitates some flexibility. There are some specifics to cover: (1) You have been born into the family of God. The Holy Scriptures speak of it as being "born again" (see John 3:1-13); (2) before this time, you had nothing in common with God because you were a sinner. But now a relationship has been established with God by your acceptance of Jesus Christ. In a sense, you are a baby in the relationship with God. As a child, you need to grow. The growth process takes place as you feed on spiritual food and this food is in the Bible (see 1 Pet. 2:2-3 and Heb. 5:13-14); (3) you receive this spiritual food by reading the Bible (see 2 Tim. 2:15 and Jer. 15:16); (4) this should be a daily occurrence. The Bible becomes a part of you as you read it, study it and memorize it (see Deut. 11:18; Josh. 1:8; Ps. 119:11).

Many camps and churches are using the *B-Rations* produced by the Navigators. This is the first of several memory booklets that have been devised and constructed for the new Christian. This includes the assurance of salvation as found in 1 John 5:11-12. The Christian life is a definite fact and not just an emotional experience. If you have received Him, He is yours.

Camps vary in their method of recording decisions, but some records should be kept. They are an aid to help camps and counselors in their follow-up program and the interest evidenced can be very meaningful for the camper. Some camps use a record form or decision card. The young person writes out the decision that he has made on two portions of the card. One portion is momentarily kept for the camp records and later sent on to the camper's church. The camper himself keeps the other portion.

Another method which has personal meaning for one of the authors is the letter. When I met Jesus Christ face-to-face at a summer conference in high school, I was asked to put in writing the decision that I made—why and what this meant to me. The letter was dated and placed in a self-addressed envelope. The camp kept this and six months later, I received a letter in the mail addressed to me in my own handwriting. Was I ever surprised to see the letter I had written that previous summer! And did it have an impact! It was a reminder of the commitment that I had personally made and it made me think, *"What am I doing about it now?"* Several years later as I was preparing for the ministry, I was sorting through some boxes and folders of materials that I had been keeping for years, and once again ran into this same letter. How precious it was to read in simple words (and poor handwriting!) the decision that changed the course of my life! I still have that letter.

While at that same camp, I had an opportunity during the closing evening service to write my testimony in the camp testimony book. I can also remember going before several hundred young people and giving my testimony. I've gone back to that book several times during the past years and what a meaningful experience that night was and continues to be. I have the assurance of new birth and can point to the time in my life when it took place.

The Assurance of Victory (1 Cor. 10:13)

Temptation is real and troublesome as evidenced by the continual questions of new and mature Christians. When a person accepts Christ, the Lord actually comes into his life in the person of the Holy Spirit. His body is the temple of the living God (1 Cor. 3:16). The Holy Spirit makes him conscious of things in his life that are contrary to what God wants. There will be temptations but God knows the capacity of his endurance and will give him the strength to overcome the temptation.

The Assurance of Forgiveness (1 John 1:9)

God tells us to confess our sins and then we have the assurance of forgiveness, no matter what the sin may have been. God wants us to realize that we have done wrong and that there is a remedy for the transgression.

The Assurance of Provision (John 16:24)

A person's joy can be full when he prays in Christ's name. As you talk with the camper, you should underscore the fact that the Christian life is not easy. It takes everything that he can give; it is a life of discipline, drive and sacrifice. The Christian life is also a life of faith (see Col. 2:6-7). A walk is merely a succession of steps and one step is taken at a time. The Christian life is the same and each step is a commitment to Jesus Christ (see Gal. 5:16,25). This life is lived by believing, just as the new birth comes by believing. A person often runs into difficulty trying to live the Christian life but finds it is possible if he trusts Christ to live through him. This life is a life of dependence upon Christ (see Ps. 62:5; Prov. 3:5-6).

Encourage and attempt to create an opportunity for the new Christian to tell someone else about his decision while he is at camp. Let him tell another camper who is a Christian, a non-Christian, one of the speakers or have him share a testimony before the entire group (see Rom. 10:9-10). Sharing before the entire camp is one of the easier places to testify. In the audience are many who have had the same experience and they are sympathetic and understand what the camper is expressing.

There must be some practical encouragement and guidance to help him face the problems that he will meet back home. Unless distance prevents, attempt to have personal contacts with the camper as often as possible. If his home is too remote, write often. Notify his home church of his decision so that it can assist him in his Christian growth. Present Bible study helps and methods to him while at camp. Work with him and establish a Bible study pattern before the conference has been completed. This will take persistence on your part. In each remaining day of camp, take time and meet with him. Encourage and show him how to study his Bible. He may sense the need but lack the method. Let him progress at his own pace and not yours.

Show him the value and method of memorizing Scripture. Assign for memory as many verses as he thinks he can learn before camp concludes. Let him know you will check on these verses each day. In addition to systematic Bible study, teach him how to pray. Pray with him and show him the importance of a regular quiet time with God. Help him make and use a prayer list.

Be careful not to exclude the older Christian from your personal attention. He, too, will profit from this individual counsel and concern. Successful counselors meet individually with each of their campers at least once during a camp. Our suggested list of helps and booklets may be beneficial:

The Basics. Published by Youth for Christ International.

Brooks, Keith L. *Teach Yourself the Bible Series.* Correspondence School, Moody Bible Institute.

Growth by Groups. Christian Outreach. Huntingdon Valley, PA.

Mattson, Lloyd. *Climbing with Christ.* Series. Guideposts, 1984.

Mears, Henrietta. *What the Bible Is All About.* Ventura, CA: Regal Books, Gospel Light Publications.

Munger, Robert. *My Heart, Christ's Home.* Downers Grove, IL: InterVarsity Press.

Quiet Time. Published by InterVarsity.

Search the Scriptures. Method of Bible Study. Billy Graham Evangelistic Association.

Studies in Christian Living. Bible Study and Scripture Memorization Program. Colorado Springs, CO: The Navigators.

Ten Basic Steps Toward Christian Maturity. Campus Crusade.

Trotman, Dawson. *Born to Reproduce.* Published by the Back to the Bible Broadcast.

These are just a few of the many published materials available. Most of these are for older teens and above, but there are several available for younger campers. Individual churches, denominations and conference grounds will have suggestions and many of their own materials. No matter what you use, be certain to establish some type of regular Bible study program with your campers. Materials such as these will be very useful.

Topical Scripture References

A. Sin

What is sin?

1 John 3:4	Transgression of the law
1 John 5:17	All unrighteousness
James 4:17	To know to do good and yet not do it
John 16:9	Unbelief

Who are sinners?

Romans 3:23	All have sinned
Isaiah 53:6	We are all like sheep
Romans 3:10	None are righteous

Result of sin

Romans 5:12	Death passes to all men
Romans 6:23	Wages of sin is death
John 8:24	You will die in your sins

God's solution

John 3:16	You will not perish but have everlasting life
1 John 5:12	He who has the Son has life
Romans 5:8	While yet sinners, Christ died for us
1 John 1:9	Confess sins, He will forgive

B. Born Again

John 3:3	Must be born again
2 Corinthians 5:17	In Christ a new creature
John 1:12	Power to become the sons of God
Galatians 2:20	New life in Christ
1 Peter 1:23	Born by the Word of God
John 3:6	New birth necessary

C. Salvation

Ephesians 2:8-9	Saved by grace through faith
John 5:24	Everlasting life by hearing and believing
Romans 5:1	Justified by faith we have peace
Acts 13:39	All who believe are justified

D. Assurance

2 Timothy 1:12	He is able to keep
1 Peter 1:5	Kept by the power of God
Philippians 1:6	Confidence in God, finishing what He started
Ephesians 2:10	We are created for good works
John 1:12	As many as received Him are sons
Romans 8:38-39	Nothing can separate us from Him

E. Dedication

Psalm 37:5	Commit your ways to the Lord
Proverbs 3:5-6	Trust in the Lord, acknowledge Him, He shall direct your paths

F. Prayer

Proverbs 15:8	The prayer of the upright is His delight so pray for one another
James 5:16	The effectual prayer of a righteous man
1 Thessalonians 5:17	Pray without ceasing

G. The Bible

Isaiah 40:8	The Word of our God shall stand forever
Ephesians 6:17	The sword of the Spirit is the Word of God

| Hebrews 4:12 | The Word of God is quick |
| 1 John 2:14 | The Word of God abides in you |

H. God

Isaiah 12:2	Behold God is my salvation
Isaiah 40:28	The Lord is the everlasting God
Philippians 2:13	For God is at work in you

I. Growing Spiritually

Ephesians 3:17-19	May Christ dwell in your hearts
Colossians 1:9-11	We do not cease to pray for you
Colossians 3:16	Let the Word of God dwell in you richly, in all wisdom
2 Timothy 2:15	Study to show yourself approved to God
1 Peter 2:2	Like newborn babies, desire the sincere milk of the Word
2 Peter 1:5-8	Supplement your faith with virtue
2 Peter 3:18	Grow in the grace and knowledge of our Lord and Saviour

J. Temptation

Isaiah 41:10	Fear not, for I am with you
1 Corinthians 10:13	There hath no temptation taken you
Philippians 1:6	He who has begun a good work in you will perform it
2 Thessalonians 3:3	But the Lord is faithful, who will establish you

Evaluating Your Counseling Experience

If you have not had much experience in the area of counseling, you may have gotten a little apprehensive as you read through this chapter. Yes, there is a great deal to learn about counseling but relax because nobody knows it all. Those who spend their lives in the field of counseling continually learn new ideas and methods. They do this first, by realizing that they still have much to learn and second, by always looking for ways in which they can improve. That is what the "Counselor-Counseling Evaluation and Training Sheet" is all about. It is nothing more than a tool to help you improve your counseling skills.

Overwhelming, you say? To some, it can appear that way. And yet when you consider that God is faithful and gives you stability, courage and the ability to realize your potential, the task becomes less frightening. Claim 2 Corinthians 4:16 *(AMP)* as your verse for comfort and reassurance as a camp counselor: "Therefore we do not become discouraged—utterly spiritless, exhausted, and wearied out through fear. Though our outer man is (progressively) decaying and wasting away, yet our inner self is being (progressively) renewed day after day." There are also two verses in Jeremiah that promise you great possibilities: "Behold, I am the Lord, the God of all flesh. Is there anything too hard for Me? Call to Me, and I will answer you, and show you great and mighty things, which you do not know" (Jer. 32:27; 33:3, *NKJV*).

Counselor—Counseling Evaluation and Training Sheet

	Yes	No	Partly—Unsure	Comments
Did you talk more than the counselee?				
What percent of the conversation was dominated by you?				
Was this person able to express what he wanted to express?				
Did you keep your mind on what he was saying or did it wander?				
Were you able to understand what he said?				
Do you feel that you were directive with him?				
Do you think he felt rejected by you?				
Did you feel like punishing him?				
Did you try to impress or shock him?				
Did you attempt to clarify the problem for him?				
If you used Scripture, did you know what Scripture to use and where to find it?				
Was the Scripture used in proper context?				
Did you have him read the Scripture?				

	Yes	No	Partly— Unsure	Comments
If prayer was a part of this time, did he pray?				
Would he want to come back and talk with you again?				
Was he able to interrupt you?				
Did he feel that he could disagree with what you said?				
Did you try to influence him as to what he should talk about?				
Were you a good listener?				
Do you feel that anything was accomplished?				
Did you push for the type of decision that you thought he should make?				
Did you seek a decision too soon?				
Did you think about things that had no connection with his problem?				
Did he feel free to say anything he wanted without fear of censure from you?				
Did you have a negative reaction to what he expressed?				
Did you feel anger or hostility toward him?				

	Yes	No	Partly— Unsure	Comments
If you did, can you determine why?				
Do you know the difference between empathy and sympathy?				
Was there a feeling of empathy present?				
Did he initiate the discussion?				
Did he take an active role in it?				
If any conclusions were drawn, did he make them and have a choice in doing so?				
Do you think that he felt he was being understood?				
Did you question him during the conversation?				
Did you use a variety of questions?				

7
Ministering to the Difficult Camper

It would be nice if you had a cabin full of well-mannered campers every time you had the opportunity to counsel at a camp. However, that would also be very unrealistic. Undoubtedly you will have some campers who are difficult to understand and control. It must be understood that ministry to unsaved children and youth will at times be very demanding and even quite frustrating. That is part of ministering to those in need. You can't always expect to have the ideal camper in your cabin.

In the event that you have an individual or perhaps even a cabin full of difficult campers, don't despair—much can be done to help you minister to these needy individuals. The purpose of this chapter is to help you get a handle on some of the difficulties you may encounter and to suggest ways to help you make the best out of a difficult situation. In some cases you can use the experience as a "teachable moment" to draw a meaningful lesson or highlight a spiritual truth. Don't look upon a difficult camper as a threat to your camping experience but rather as a stepping stone for further growth and development. As you encounter these individuals you will find your counseling skills improving and your wisdom growing. Soon other counselors will be coming to you for advice on how to handle a difficult camper.

Home Environment Influences

John is a new camper this year. He has never been away from home before and he is giving his counselor fits! He is constantly in trouble. If he doesn't get his own way or has a dispute with another camper, he simply lashes out in a fit of anger and hits the other person. He seems very tense and can't talk out these disagreements. When he is approached about his difficulties with others, he feels there wasn't anything wrong with settling disputes his way. Why would a young person act like this?

Investigation reveals that the source of John's problem goes back to his home environment. His parents are constantly fighting and arguing. There hasn't been love in this home for some time. From time to time the parents separate, but then reunite and try to get along. This is done primarily for economic reasons. They are very hostile toward one another and physical violence is a part of every day.

John lives in an atmosphere of stress and tension. He has little opportunity at home to see people solve problems aside from the use of force and physical pressure so he fights and uses physical force because this is all he knows; it is merely his way of solving a problem. Perhaps this is acceptable behavior at home, but it isn't at camp. Before you judge why a person misbehaves at camp, know the motivation behind the action.

You as a counselor are in a position to influence the campers during an important time in their lives. The problems that you face are those of having people from diverse homes and varied backgrounds. You will have to adjust to each one and enable them to adjust to one another and the camp program. Habits which have been entrenched over the years will be hard to break, but you still have a responsibility to help the individuals. Some will need to change their behavior patterns and attitudes and will attempt to do so, but won't make very much progress. You'll have to learn how to reach each camper and influence his conduct. You will also need to understand the "why" of his behavior.

Why do campers misbehave? This is a question all counselors ask at one time or another. There are a number of suggested reasons that can be presented. Remember that some campers may have these motivations and many others may not. Each one may have a different drive that causes him to behave in the manner that he does. You want to know the reason for the act. You are interested in why things are done.

Common behavior cases can be classified into three categories:

1. *The excessively inhibited person.* This is the camper who is very tense and inwardly nervous, but outwardly conforms. Why? Because this is the only way he feels he can gain approval. Often this is because his parents are cold, critical individuals and their favor has to be won. Generally, he presents few or no problems, but often he is worse off than the one who lashes out and is overt in his misbehavior.

2. *The excessively uninhibited person.* Basically, this camper is unsocialized and you know when he is present! Many are aggressive and have great difficulty achieving good interpersonal relations. They are in constant conflict with others. The behavior that you see is a symptom of their problems.

3. *The well-adjusted person.* This camper is an acceptable and loyal member of his own group. Basically, he maintains good interpersonal relations.

Rudolf Dreikurs presents a different theory in his book, *Children: The Challenge.*[1] He believes that many children pursue "mistaken goals." The first of these is the desire for undue attention. Many discouraged children use this to help them feel that they belong. The second mistaken goal is the struggle for power. This comes about because of a clash or conflict between a child and adult. The child disobeys to exert his power and won't conform to a higher power. When the power contest is intensified, some children choose the third goal which is retaliation and revenge. The fourth mistaken goal is generally chosen by a discouraged child. He attempts to demonstrate his complete inadequacy. He gives up entirely and takes a helpless attitude. This helplessness enables him to avoid unpleasant tasks. For a complete and thorough discussion of these goals and methods of working with them, we encourage you to read *Children: The Challenge.*

There are divergent theories concerning the cause of various behaviors. The most accepted and recognized will be discussed here. Every person has emotional needs and requirements that last a lifetime.

Basic Camper Needs

What are these basic needs? First of all, *there must be affection and acceptance*. When this is present, there is a sense of inner contentment or of well being. Acceptance involves feeling wanted by others and belonging to a home and family—even to a dorm at a weekend camp. We need to be able to share our thoughts and feelings with others, to let our hair down and be completely honest, and to experience others liking us when we are this way. The feeling of love must be conveyed; this is the basic need.

People also have a need for power. This is the desire to show or feel power over something or someone. This drive can be directed and the need fulfilled when a camper derives satisfaction from the making of a pair of moccasins in the craft hut, completing a 10-mile hike or mastering the jack-knife dive at the pool. This can also be achieved by performing one's job well on a camp council. Misdirected or displaced power creates the bully, the disobedient, the stubborn or the camper who exhibits temper tantrums. This can also be evidenced in lying, dawdling and procrastinating.

The drive for security is another basic need that we all experience. Many campers will miss the security of home when they first come to camp and their reactions will be varied.

There is also *the drive for recognition and achievement*. The camper needs to develop the conviction that he can accomplish something and that he is adequate enough to meet life head-on. At the same time, he needs others to see and recognize that he can accomplish something in this life.

These wishes or drives are present in every camper as they are present in all normal people. They do, however, vary in intensity. Recognizing that these are fundamental drives may help you understand and interpret more correctly camper behavior. The well-adjusted person seeks to satisfy these in socially acceptable ways, but when the person becomes frustrated or feels that he isn't satisfying them, he often resorts to unapproved devices.

Hierarchy of Camper Needs

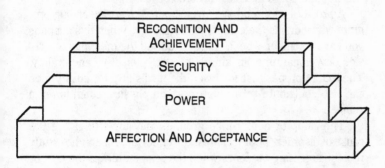

Causes of Camper Misbehavior

Certain campers will attempt to fulfill these needs at the expense of others. We need to listen, hear and watch so that we can sense and understand what our campers are feeling. Many times misbehavior means that the camper has some current unsatisfied emotional needs or that he is expressing hurt, anger or fear because needs weren't met in his past. Try, as much as possible in the limited amount of time available, to help satisfy those needs.

Other problems can come about because of the counselor himself. The relationship between you and the camper is crucial. See that the campers are satisfied and adjusting to the program. Your attempt to force adult values or adherence to plans and procedures will initiate agitation. Resentment against over-severe, or worse than that, inconsistent discipline in camp will develop into misbehavior.

Boredom, idleness or too much energy with too little to do will be evidenced by mischievous behavior. Boredom must not be thought of just in terms of not having anything to do and a lack of interesting activities. This is basic to becoming bored, but other factors influence the camper: Forcing him to participate in an activity that isn't to his liking, frustration because of inadequate and unadaptable equipment and a military type of schedule will create a bored and disinterested camper.

A problem on the other extreme is the over-demanding program which drains the camper of his energy. When this happens you have a camper who falls asleep during the meetings or fireside devotional time, making him overly sensitive and crabby. The lack of proper rest following the meals or poor quality food can also contribute to the deteriorated physical condition of a camper.

The camp or conference grounds may unwittingly be the cause of disorder. Poor facilities, uncomfortable seats, hot stuffy rooms, a meeting outdoors when the temperature is too cold or windy, poor lighting, not enough room and distractive noises will hamper the progress of the camp. These, however, will usually create just minor disturbances such as restlessness, talking, inattention and drowsiness.

Other campers may experience fear, rejection or isolation in an overwhelming crowd. Fear may be caused by the lack of familiar surroundings or by being away from the security of home, church and friends. Be sensitive to the feelings of a camper, as we never know what remark by others will give him the feeling of being rejected.

One camper may feel like a displaced person because of the numbers at camp or in his dorm; he isn't used to this type of close living. Another may feel rejected because of a basic feeling and attitude of inferiority. This may be centered in an actual handicap and slow development. It may also be an unfounded fear, but just as real to the camper as one based on fact.

Some of your most pressing problems may come from Church or Christian homes. Quite often these campers react against authority and their faith as they haven't had any opportunity to express their doubts and raise the questions that have been plaguing them for years. Because they were brought up within the Church, they have adhered to an expected behavior pattern and have developed a spiritual facade with no internalization of the Christian values. Others from this group will react as a way of showing their independence and resentment against their church or parents.

Following is a list of some of the camp behavior problems you may encounter: the timid or lonesome camper, the coward, the hypochondriac, the nervous camper, the bed wetter, the sissy, the seclusive person, the daydreamer, the liar, the overly dependent, the unresponsive, the lethargic, the selfish, the stubborn, the restless or the overactive.

Some will have habits of poor eating, sleeping, speech, nail biting, thumb sucking and masturbation. Still others will exhibit traits that include teasing, bullying, fighting, stealing, showing off, temper tantrums, disobedience, destructiveness, swearing, sexual problems, over-critical, faultfinding and the know-it-all. There will also be those who won't follow peer leadership.

This is not the end of the world, nor is it the most pleasant counseling experience you will ever have. When one of these rears its head you must handle it. Hopefully, the suggestions presented within this book will enable you to work with these problems.

Withdrawn and Seclusive Campers

Milton Milquetoast

First, meet Milton Milquetoast. He appears to be timid. He avoids contact with others at camp and seems to retreat from everyone and every activity. Far too often, counselors are pleased to find this quiet, unobtrusive camper, but Milton can be a very serious problem. His actions may take the form of just withdrawing from camp life and staying to himself. Walking by himself, doing crafts alone, daydreaming, hanging back and watching, disappearing for a time or staying in the cabin may be the pattern for Milton. Why would he act this way? What makes him behave like this? Some daydreams offer more satisfaction than the real life experiences.

He may feel sorry for himself and retreat into his own private world to nurse his wounds and hurts. He may retreat because of a physical deficiency that is too obvious to be comfortable. Perhaps he has been so overprotected in his home environment that his social development has been stifled, even retarded, and he simply doesn't relate well with others in a group. Withdrawing may just be a temporary solution. He can't converse with others in his own peer group. Perhaps this is the first time away from home. He may be dominated at home and thrust into a subjective position. Now he finds it hard to break out of this mold.

In some cases he is less mature or hasn't been to camp before and is overwhelmed with all that he sees taking place. He finds it hard adjusting to everything. It is much safer and easier to retreat than to attempt to break into the busy, eventful life.

Perhaps there is some fear of the opposite sex involved which is of so much concern to him that it hampers his total social development. He may withdraw because of unfavorable experiences in the past, either at school, home or camp. He doesn't want to take the risk of getting hurt again. Perhaps it was a counselor who did this or perhaps he is afraid of you as his counselor! What can you do to help this situation?

1. See if there are any records available at the camp or in the physical report in the nurse's office. Information gained here may shed some light on his behavior.

2. Attempt to find the underlying reason(s) for his reaction.

3. Make sure that he is a part of the group and provide him with things to do with other campers who will take an interest in him and accept him just the way he is.

4. Show a sincere interest and concern for him yourself. Remember, this doesn't mean to give sympathy; be a friend to him.

5. Provide some opportunity for the two of you to get together; encourage him to talk about himself. This may come about through participating in an activity that will provide him with some enjoyment.

6. Attempt to find a group project or a situation where he can be a part. Perhaps he has a latent skill that needs developing. This can be a source of satisfaction for him and the encouragement and recognition that he derives from others will build his confidence. When he feels that he can make a contribution, he will start to construct his sense of confidence. When you do give him something to do, make sure that it is something at which he can succeed.

7. In sports or athletic competition, place emphasis on the sportsmanship rather than on winning. Avoid methods of selecting teams that will embarrass him because he isn't picked or because he is the last one to be taken—and reluctantly at that! Try to assign groups and teams equally. When recognition is given to campers, it can be given to those who have achieved just a little as well as to those who are accustomed to winning because of their physical prowess.

8. Your discussion time with the campers can be used in such a way that he learns to sense and cope with problems. The final stage is to develop an understanding of the reasons for his actions and then develop ways of helping one another in a spirit of Christian love.

9. If he withdraws because of unfounded fear, a discussion letting him air his feelings may lead to a better and more logical understanding of the situation.

Sally Solo

Closely associated with Milton Milquetoast is Sally Solo. Loneliness is a pathetic feeling and one of isolation and futility in its severest forms. It is quite natural for the shy or timid person to be lonely. The causes for this will again vary, but homesickness can contribute to it. The inability to find things of interest in camp, lack of close friends, missing those back home, fear of new friends and of the rough camping situation contribute to this feeling of being lonely. Enabling her to "talk it out" may conquer the first hurdle and prepare the road for a different direction on her part. Putting her into group activities in which she is proficient will help to raise her morale and feelings of self-confidence.

Harley Homebody

The never-ending problem of homesickness is something that occurs in varying degrees at most camps. It is a longing for the nearness of someone or something that is very close or important to the camper. It can be recognized in campers like Harley Homebody. He withdraws or mopes around camp, shows a lack of participation, cries and is sullen. Sometimes he openly states that he is homesick and wants to leave camp this very instant! Perhaps you are surprised that anyone would want to leave the beautiful and refreshing surroundings of any camp to go back to the congestion and hurried pace of life in the cities and suburbs. There are reasons for this feeling and to Harley, it can be a powerful drive.

Quite often, there has been an over attachment between him and his parents. Overindulgence and protection at home doesn't develop self-confidence and they've been afraid to let go and let grow. This relationship can still be nurtured while he is at camp by incessant calls and letters from his parents. The attachment back home may be to special friends and this occurs, not only with the juniors but with the teens. The involvement with boy and girl friends can dominate his total life perspective at this stage. In some cases, he has been so strongly attached to pets or club programs that the thought of missing these appears to be too much for him!

The camp itself will have some effect upon homesickness. Strange surroundings, the lack of making Harley feel at home or the lack of interest in him will be a detriment. The new atmosphere may also contribute to a feeling of insecurity. If he is self-conscious about himself in any way, homesickness is an easy way out of the predicament. For some, this is the first experience in a group situation and the limited privacy or complete lack of it may be upsetting. Homesickness for some may come when things don't go as they had anticipated. Also any lack in the environment that leaves a need unfulfilled may precipitate this feeling.

In many camps and conferences, there are a number of campers who have been sent to camp against their will. Parents either feel that this will be a wonderful educational experience for their child or else it is the most convenient way to have a vacation away from their offspring. Shipping them off to camp erases their conscience about wanting them away for a period of time. It has been noted that homesickness doesn't always show itself at the start of a camp but more toward the third or fourth day and particularly around mealtime—and it can be contagious!

What is the basic underlying reason for homesickness? The one word that can sum up this emotion is fear! Simple fear is disturbing and, if allowed to grow and develop, can become a very disrupting emotion involving the surroundings, the camp, the people and the activities.

What can you do as his counselor? If you are counseling for your own church you may be able to ascertain in advance who your campers will be and arrange to meet them at your church. Call them and get acquainted before the camp begins. The interest you show at this time will help your relationships later on.

If you are unable to take this approach before the camp, lay groundwork at the beginning so this problem doesn't develop. Welcome each camper as soon as he arrives. Some camps have welcome signs in the dorm and name tags ready to be pinned on the minute the camper steps into camp. An attractive and homey cabin will add to the desire to stay and make this his home for a time.

The best method is to make each one feel wanted and loved and accepted as a part of the group. You may have to assist him in establishing new friendships. Perhaps you know of one in the cabin who is an old-timer to camping, or perhaps he has the same interest or hobby as this potential homesick fatality. A buddy system may help to get all campers involved quickly.

Be alert for possible signs of this malady. If you have a fellow or girl who tends to go off by himself you may have cause to wonder, especially if this takes place during mealtime or the evening hours.

Physical symptoms or problems like constipation, indigestion or diarrhea are contributing factors. Any type of illness can initiate homesick feelings. The warmth and care that he is used to at home may be missed. If you can get him to stay just one more day or two until that special swim meet is held, he will more than likely remain for the duration of camp. Help him to talk about his feelings.

One of the best ways you can help a camper with one of the first three challenges is to show a special interest. However, in the process of doing this you may discover one who over-responds to this type of treatment by becoming your shadow. If this happens you have discovered our next profile.

Carl Clinger

Some camp counselors have referred to Carl Clinger as the "counselor's pet," not because this is your desire and plan but because he has so attached himself to you. He hangs around, even bothers or pesters you. He follows you everywhere and anywhere, even to the bathroom. In many cases, he is trying very hard to please you. He does this because of lack of acceptance by others at camp and in his home. He is trying too hard and you may have to combat your own feelings of impatience, dislike and aversion to him.

This is also the pattern for others who show some interest in him. He tries so hard that people shun him. Because of his forward thrust, he drives people away from him. Ignoring or avoiding his attentions won't work. Perhaps if you get him to work with others, this will help the situation and keep him from hanging around you. Too often, however, this won't solve the problem, for as soon as he has completed his task, he'll be right back.

He may need someone to be very frank with him and tell him what he is doing. Let him know that you like him and accept him but that he doesn't have to be around you so much to keep your favor. Indicate to him that he is actually missing out on a good time by not being involved with the others in the cabin. Guide him into some activity. Don't push him onto the others as they probably have some of the initial feelings that you have experienced, too.

Dawn Daydreamer

Daydreaming is natural to most people and has some positive value, but Dawn Dreamer spends her time in reverie and prefers to sit alone and daydream rather than participate in the interpersonal and sports activities. Excessive daydreaming can be unhealthy. When too much time is devoted to this and the camper would rather daydream than establish contacts with children or young people, he has a problem. Your friendship and counsel here may open the door to the reason behind this behavior. Encourage and assist him to break into the group activities.

Summary Chart of Withdrawn and Seclusive Campers

	Profile Characteristics	Steps Toward Resolution of Behavior
Milton Milquetoast	Timid appearance Avoids contact with others Retreats from social events Spends hours by himself Prefers to be last on hikes Does crafts without help Daydreams during free time Stays in the cabin Sometimes can't be found	1. Examine any records for history/patterns 2. Attempt to find any underlying reasons 3. Get other campers to interact with him 4. Show a sincere interest in him 5. Seek out opportunities for one-on-one contact 6. Get him involved in a group project 7. Emphasize sportsmanship, not winning 8. Seek to understand the reasons for his actions; develop a "we" attitude

Sally Solo	Timid appearance Excessive shyness Potentially homesick Lack of close friends Fear of new friendships Cries without know reason	1. Encourage her to talk about it 2. Get involved in group activities 3. Get other campers to interact with her 4. Seek one-on-one opportunities 5. Establish a project with her
Harley Home-body	Homesick Long periods of depression Cries often Sulks, mopes around camp Lack of desire for fun Withdraws from activities May be over-protected at home Fear of unknown Constipation, indigestion	1. Help camper get oriented 2. Get involved in activities 3. Help him gain new friends 4. Don't let him sit alone for long 5. Make campers feel welcome and loved 6. Establish a buddy system for him 7. Talk about special events to come 8. Speak about "extended" activities 9. Provide an atmosphere of acceptance

Carl Clinger	The counselor's "pet" Becomes your shadow at camp Pesters the counselors Smothers you with friendship Fears rejection of others	1. Help him make other friends at camp 2. Establish a buddy system for him 3. Get him involved in projects with others 4. Introduce him to others at camp 5. Let him know why you like him 6. Tell him he doesn't have to be so close 7. Don't push him onto others
Dawn Day-dreamer	Excessive day-dreaming Prefers to be left alone Lacks friends at camp Perhaps feeling homesick Avoids peer interaction Shuns others in cabin Requires prodding to eat	1. Get involved in activities 2. Establish peer relations 3. Get him involved in projects 4. Determine their interests, hobbies 5. Take them on individual activities, i.e. sailing, canoeing, hiking 6. Develop mutual interests

Overt and Demonstrative Campers

The Wise Guy

These behavioral problems are marked by withdrawing and seclusiveness. There are situations on the other side of the ledger, too. Campers who are wise guys or show offs are in attendance just as much as the others. Some attempt to dominate all the activities and appoint themselves leader in everything. This occurs even when other campers protest and are quite vocal in their reactions toward him.

The Sleeper

Once in a while you may meet a "sleeper." This camper has leadership potential but it has lain dormant for years or has had no avenue of expression available. Now he makes an attempt but because of a lack of experience and security, he blunders and gropes around. If the camper doesn't receive the attention that he is seeking from this behavior, it loses its impetus and significance. Confront him with his behavior. Explore with him why he thinks that he behaves in this manner. This will bring the problem into focus. It may reveal to you many inner feelings and stimulate needed hours of counseling with him. If there are areas where he is proficient, provide him with natural and needed outlets where this skill can be exhibited, used, and praised. If he is as good as he thinks he is in some area, leadership recognition will come to him.

Competence in any area must fit the needs and interest of his fellow campers. Perhaps the sleeper has been limited and stifled in his range of interests back home. The home or community could have been lacking in its environmental stimuli and opportunities. Now, with the abundance of resources available to you at camp, the possibility of broadening his interest is possible. New recreational activities and athletic events, wildlife, crafts, music and your personal interest may open new horizons heretofore untouched and unthought.

The Know-It-All

Some campers try to over demonstrate their talents

(whether real or imaginary) and a few criticize constantly. Others talk continually and never let anyone else speak his piece. The "know-it-all" attitude is one that is offensive and elicits negative reactions. A lack in patience on your part will make you see this as an action that needs punishment or discipline. But in reality this behavior is exhibiting an inner need and lack. You may have seen adults like this, schoolmates or working associates who fit this description. The following example may point out how the know-it-all camper can be helped.

A young counselor was having difficulty controlling some of the boys in his cabin. They were noisy, didn't want to attend the meetings and had skipped the morning service. Now the boys were all in the cabin talking and laying plans for their next escapade. One older boy, Dave, appeared to be influencing most of the others. The last day or so he had become sarcastic to those in authority. As the counselor stepped into the room, he heard Dave tell the others that there wasn't anything to worry about as no one would catch them and even if they did, nothing would happen to them.

The counselor stepped forward and asked where the boys were during the last meeting and why they hadn't attended. The group fell silent except for Dave who stood his ground and said defiantly, "We didn't feel like coming and we may not attend the one tonight. What are you going to do about it? You can't make us!" The other fellows, upon hearing this outburst, seemed to find their courage and echoed Dave. They were encouraging him and at the same time delighting in this contest between their cabin mate and counselor. How would you have handled this power struggle?

Fortunately the counselor, young as he was, had the presence of mind to remove Dave from the group and take him out of earshot of the rest. Had he continued this discussion and discipline in front of the entire cabin of boys, little would have been accomplished. When Dave was alone and didn't have the encouragement and strength from the others, he was a different person and could be talked to in a sensible manner. At the same time, the boys were much more subdued, even obedient, without their leader present.

The problem was overcome and better understanding developed between all of the fellows and the counselor. If faced with a similar situation, remove the one antagonist from the group when you talk with him. This is basic policy when dispensing a discipline or a reprimand. Give the person the courtesy of privacy.

Aggressiveness is a very forceful emotion and one that threatens others when they come into contact with it. Again, you may have campers who are overly aggressive. Many counselors experience great feelings of inadequacy when they encounter an aggressive camper. Insecurity and a lack of love, perhaps, has bred feelings of hostility and anger toward others. In an attempt to reduce tension, the camper may be unable to cope with his frustration and resort to aggressive behavior. The effectiveness of this is only temporary and the need is still present. Its forms are many and varied.

The Braggart

You perhaps have encountered the braggart, bully, tough or bossy guy. This individual excels, or attempts to, by domineering others, talking too much, taking and using other's belongings, fighting or swearing.

Aggressiveness can take the opposite form, however, and a person can be very aggressive by assuming a passive role. Some have called or labeled this reaction the passive-aggressive role. The person who says that he didn't hear you, delays others or finds ways to irritate people in subtle ways fits this category. Quite often, we fail to recognize some of these reactions as being aggressive. We tend to react more to the outwardly aggressive type. How can you counsel with the person who is a braggart?

A kind, friendly attitude toward him (even when he has dominated others) will break through his veneer and impress upon him that you care about him. He needs someone to care. Help him to establish some friendships and to find some place in the group where he can be accepted. If he can be praised for acceptable behavior and for deeds that are exceptional, this will help.

When braggarts experience approval for socially acceptable behavior, their need has been fulfilled and they are on the way to learning a better and more effective pattern.

Counselors have been overheard to remark that they have a camper who is never quiet in action or word. He seems to fight constantly and is hyperactive. If you are confronted with a camper like this, take notice. Some fidgetiness is natural, but an excessive amount indicates generally an unhappy person who is troubled and does not know how to meet or deal with the emotional problems that trouble him. These campers are always in motion: squirming, wiggling, fiddling or playing with objects. If fingernails are chewed or bitten, this is one good indication that not all is well within. A child or adolescent who is fidgety likes to keep busy, but often the hyperactive child should have his schedule altered from very strenuous activities to the less active. Slowing the person down, but keeping him occupied, may have a quieting effect upon him.

The Bed Wetter

Another common problem, particularly with juniors, is that of enuresis or bed-wetting. This is something that happens with almost every child at one age or another. With some, the behavior is carried over much later than with others. There can be several factors causing this, including physical factors, nervousness or overactivity. It will be to your benefit to check the camper's health record before the first night to see if any have indicated this problem. Other reasons for the problem are lack of early and consistent training in the home, past illness where the person has spent a great deal of time in bed and drinking too much liquid near bedtime. Most causes, however, tend to be psychological and indicate an inability to satisfy some of his needs.

If you have a camper such as this, you may want to take some basic precautions such as using a rubber sheet on the bed. If bunk beds are used, place this camper on a bottom bunk. Limiting liquids after dinner is necessary and be sure that the person uses the rest room before going to bed. Some advocate awakening the person 30 minutes to an hour after retiring and having him go to the rest room again. Don't allow the others to ridicule or haze the camper.

The Thief

A problem that is difficult to contend with, whether it occurs at camp or at school, is that of stealing. When stealing occurs, people react quickly and perhaps too severely. Most deal solely with the behavioral aspect instead of the cause. The nature of the problem can vary, depending upon the age of the camper and the particular situation. The act can also vary from a one-time proposition to a compulsive disorder in which the value of the object is of little importance to the person involved. The act itself can be the significant factor. This type of behavior, if brought out into the open, can result in strained relationships between campers and even physical disagreements.

As is the case with other deviations, the causes are many, but each is important. One reason may be an undeveloped sense of possession. In some cases with campers who come from a materially deprived environment, this may be an acceptable form of behavior. Seeing other campers with possessions that are of greater value and worth, the young person sometimes steals in order to join the group of the "haves" instead of the "have-nots."

In some situations, the act of stealing is a cry for help in that he seeks and craves attention—a need not being fulfilled. This is one sure way to get others to sit up and take notice of him.

Another may resort to stealing because the parents haven't allowed him to have sufficient money of his own to spend as he sees fit. This drives him to obtain, no matter the means.

Some stealing falls into the categories of reaction, rebellion against authority or a way of getting back at either a camper or staff member. When campers have deep psychological problems, the overt behavior can take many forms and stealing may be one of them.

From these causes, it can be stated that you must be careful in dealing with the theft situation as, too often, emotions become aroused when the camper is apprehended or discovered.

In cases involving stealing, it is important to consult with the senior counselor or the boy's or girl's dean, as the case may be. Endeavoring to find out the reason for the behavior must be done in a slow, patient manner with understanding and love. Many campers, when confronted, may retreat into a shell and be uncommunicative. If the camper feels that nothing but punitive measures are forthcoming, he will resist. It may be necessary to indicate the probable reasons for his behavior to him so he can properly understand his own motivation.

Every effort should be expended to encourage him to develop self-control and here is another area that can be entrusted to Christ. If there are associates in the camp who have been contributing factors to his problem, make certain these campers are confronted and helped. Seek to keep the detrimental influences separated.

Periodic checks on the camper's behavior and relations with others may be necessary but must be done in a spirit of helping and support, rather than of suspicion. If others in the group are affected, let them know that the situation has been handled and those involved properly corrected.

The assistance of the group may have to be cultivated in order to ensure the proper atmosphere in the cabin and to help the camper in question. Any materials taken or used should be restored and repaid. In some instances, the camp director may ask the parents to come to camp and discuss the matter. Any corrective measures should be meaningful to the camper. Your goal in this should be one of benefit and one that is constructive.

The Loose Mouth

Language is another concern, for foul language and swearing is not tolerated at Christian camps. When you run abruptly into this, the typical response is to react quickly, definitely, and let the person know this is not acceptable. Furthermore, one more time will be his undoing! This usually succeeds in stopping the outbursts, but the camper will just be a little wiser and more careful about the next instance and there will be one—you can count on that! Campers expect this and when confronted, it makes little impression upon them because they have experienced this reaction before.

One counselor had a unique way of dealing with the problem. One day he came upon a couple of campers talking who weren't aware of anyone else in the vicinity. Their language was rich with descriptive adjectives and four-letter words. The boys looked up as the counselor approached. He smiled and said, "Hi fellows," and they replied rather hesitantly and sheepishly, "Hi." "By the way," the counselor said, "I couldn't help but overhear you as I walked up and I was wondering if you could tell me what those last two words mean." The boys looked a little surprised and stammered out, "Er, uh, what words?" "Oh, you know which ones. I've heard a number of fellows use them and I just was wondering, since *you* used them, if you could tell me what they mean. Most people know what a word means when they use it." "Well, uh, well we just said them I guess. I don't know if we thought what they meant or anything. I guess it's because other guys use them and we didn't think anyone else would hear us."

These two boys were a little taken aback as they were confronted in a much different manner about their abusive language. This counselor had used this technique many times and found that it opened the door to discussions as to why a person uses foul language. He wins a hearing when the campers realize that they're not going to be scolded and lectured about what they have done. They find that they can talk with someone about the reason for using the words.

Words that refer to sex or the sexual relationship in some way are often used with complete misunderstanding. The ensuing conversation, if built upon the above approach, can lead into a very natural and profitable discussion about sex. Many of the misconceptions can be cleared up.

In any of the problems concerning swearing or abusive language, the Scriptures can be introduced to provide a clear presentation of God's view of sex. This can be shared so that wholesome attitudes concerning sex can begin or be reinforced.

Summary Chart of Overt and Demonstrative Campers

	Profile Characteristics	Steps Toward Resolution of Behavior
The Wise Guy	Show-off attitude Attempts to dominate others Appoints himself "leader" Autocratic personality Talks constantly	1. Have patience with him 2. Confront this behavior 3. Remove from peers at meetings if he becomes disruptive
The Sleeper	Dormant leadership potential Lacks security, experience May "cut up" and disobey	1. Provide leadership opportunities 2. Guide in leadership skill development 3. Confront this behavior if needed 4. Allow his input for decisions
The Know-It-All	Instigates pranks A leader in the cabin Manipulates peer behavior Disregard for authority	1. Isolate from peers 2. Explain rationale for rules, policies 3. Seek their help, participation 4. Provide limited leadership experiences

The Braggart	The camp bully Picks fights with others Uses his physical advantage Passive-aggressive behavior	1. Be kind, friendly and accepting 2. Be firm in your leadership patterns 3. Praise acceptable behavior 4. Slow his activity
The Bed Wetter	Nervousness or overactivity Insecurity at home Perhaps a past illness Too many fluids too late	1. Examine health records on first day 2. Put camper on lower bunk 3. Limit fluid intake after dinner 4. Protect his dignity
The Thief	Undeveloped sense of his possessions Materially deprived Envious of others Rebellion of authority	1. Consult with the camp's dean 2. Help him understand severity of the crime 3. Encourage development of self-control 4. Seek peer/parental assistance
The Loose Mouth	Associates with wise guys and braggarts Poorly directed leader Insecure and fearful	1. Be tactful in your approach 2. Ask for explanation of words 3. Don't avoid/fear confrontation 4. Seek meaningful discussions

It isn't uncommon to find that children or teenagers can give us insight concerning proper ways of working with them. Consider these suggestions from the lips of a child.

Memos from Your Playground Child

1. Don't be afraid to be firm with me. I prefer it; it makes me feel more secure.

2. Don't let me form bad habits. I have to rely on you to detect them in the early stages.

3. Don't make me feel smaller than I am. It only makes me behave stupidly "big."

4. Don't correct me in front of others if you can help it. I'll take much more notice if you talk quietly with me in private.

5. Don't make me feel that my mistakes are sins. It upsets my sense of values.

6. Don't always protect me from the consequences. I need to learn the painful way sometimes.

7. Don't be upset when I say, "I hate you." It isn't you I hate, but your being a symbol of authority.

8. Don't take too much notice of my small complaints. At times they bring the attention I need.

9. Don't nag. If you do, I shall have to protect myself by appearing deaf.

10. Don't make rash promises. Remember that I feel badly let down when promises are broken.

11. Don't forget I cannot explain myself as well as I should like. That's why I'm not always accurate.

12. Don't tax my honesty too much. I am easily frightened into telling lies.

13. Don't be inconsistent. That completely confuses me and makes me lose faith in you.

14. Don't put me off when I ask questions. If you do, you will find that I stop asking and seek my information elsewhere.

15. Don't ever suggest that you are perfect or infallible. It gives me too great a shock when I discover that you are neither.

16. Don't tell me my fears are silly. They are terribly real and you can do much to reassure me if you try to understand.

17. Don't ever think it is beneath your dignity to apologize to me. An honest apology makes me feel surprisingly warm toward you.

18. Don't forget I love experimenting. I couldn't get on without it, so please put up with it.

19. Don't forget that I can't strive without lots of understanding, but I don't need to tell you, do I?[2]

Questions for Further Study

1. Of the two major groups presented—withdrawing and seclusive or overt and demonstrative—which type of camper will be most challenging for you to counsel? Why?
2. Which type of individual would you have been at the age of 10?
3. What will you do if you have several like Milton, Carl and Harley in your cabin?
4. Do you feel you possess enough self-confidence to discipline a camper like "The Thief" or "The Loose Mouth"?
5. At what point should you go and seek the help of the dean?
6. What other resources do you have access to in order to help maintain control in your cabin?
7. How would sharing your needs with other counselors at camp help you as you counsel some of these difficult campers?
8. How could your personality affect the way you respond to some of these campers? Is it possible that you may need to make some changes too? If so, what kinds? How will you make them?

8
Contemporary Issues in Camp Counseling

Much has happened in our world during the past few decades which has contributed to a changing society here in North America. The decade of the '60s brought about a rise in social unrest, apathy and anti-government sentiment. The '70s can be characterized as a decade of escape. Youth ran away from the pressures of their world by experimenting with drugs and alcohol. Many of them turned to cult movies and rock music as an attempt to "tune out" the world around them. In the '80s we are seeing a rise in materialism among adolescents. Along with materialism is the influence of rock videos and personal superficiality. These are but a few of the many issues that have contributed to the shaping of our present youth culture.

Because of the influence of these contemporary social tides, it is only natural that many of these issues will show themselves in the lives of campers. It is for this reason that we will deal with many of the contemporary issues encountered at camp today: the camper from a broken home, the urban community, the abused camper and the juvenile delinquent.

It is also our intention to provide you with some materials which will aid you in your understanding of these unique counseling needs.

Counseling the Camper from a Broken Home

It is unfortunate that so many of our campers are coming from broken homes. The rise in the divorce rate across America has occurred in unprecedented proportions. One in every two marriages will end in divorce today. This has resulted in a corresponding increase in the number of children of divorce—over one million new children each year. In 1982 the Census Bureau reported that one quarter of all the children in the United States are members of single parent families.

When a parent leaves the home it sets in motion a series of adjustments and emotional transitions for the child. At a point in time when the adolescent is experiencing enormous change already, a divorce in the family compounds the trauma.

It is very common for parents to send their children off to camp during the week the father or mother will be moving out of the home. The parents believe it will be easier on the child if he returns and finds the transition has already begun. The difficulty with this situation is that the camp must deal with the emotional shock that the child faces. Many children know that one of their parents is moving out and they want to be there to say their good-byes and help where possible. Counselors at camp are left with the responsibility of calming their fears and reassuring them of a stable future. This is difficult to do when the counselor knows little, if anything, about the family background.

The Camper

The profile of a camper who comes from a divorced family may vary depending on how long ago the divorce occurred. If it is a recent divorce the camper may be experiencing mood swings, guilt, depression and long periods of intense isolation. The child may also express feelings of hostility and aggression. He may even exhibit the same behavior that would be expected if one of his parents had died. With the death of a parent there is a final letting go of the loved one. In the case of a divorced parent there is never that finality. As a result there are feelings of confusion and turmoil. It is common for camp counselors to feel inadequate in their ability to meet the camper's needs. A closer look at those needs may assist the counselor in this important responsibility.

His Needs

The camper needs someone available for him to speak with whenever the need arises. He needs friendships and a loyal listener. Feelings of rejection must be resolved. The guilt that the divorce has brought needs to be a high priority in your counseling. Although they may not express it in those terms, guilt is a very common feeling on the part of children of divorced parents. They need routine activities to compensate for the feeling that everything is falling apart in their world. These campers will want personal attention and a wise counselor will recognize this desire before the camper resigns to deviant behavior to attain it. The loss of self-confidence can be overcome to some degree by affirming the camper's activities and accomplishments. If the camper is extremely anxious, due to the recency of the divorce, a call home may help to calm his apprehensions. Use caution in this, however, because it is possible that a phone call can have a compounding effect on the life of the camper.

How You Can Help

Ministry to the camper from a broken home should first be directed as guilt resolution. If the camper is experiencing guilt he should be directed to the source of forgiveness. You may not be able to convince the child that the divorce is not his fault but you can provide the camper with a solution to his dilemma. Guide the camper to the verses of Scripture which teach peace and forgiveness based upon an attitude of confession. Before any constructive growth can occur it is important to deal with this important issue.

You can also assist the camper from a broken home by providing him with a great deal of love and reassurance. Such statements as, "I'm sure your parents still love you," "You will always be your parents' child," "You are not the only one who has gone through this," "It isn't your fault," "I know there is a lot of pain now but it won't hurt so much as time goes by," "You are not alone in this problem," "I want you to know that I care," will help reassure the camper of your concern and friendship. An arm around the shoulder can also speak a thousand words at the right time. A gentle smile and warm touch can do wonders to give the camper reassurance, too.

A good stable environment can, to a large degree, assist the child from a broken home. His life is in a state of turmoil and uncertainty. By providing the camper with a consistent life-style you will do much to calm his fears and anxiety. Try and get the camper involved in activities which will take his mind off the current problems at home. He needs to have his attention drawn toward carefree activities like swimming, horseback riding, archery, sailing, etc. Even a craft project can be a helpful activity as it may provide you with an opportunity to discuss the situation while still keeping busy. When the camper is faced with several hours of uninterrupted time to reflect, he may pursue critical thinking that leads to a downward spiral of emotional hurt.

The most important thing you can do for a camper from a broken home is be his friend. Don't try and play the part of a therapist. Just reach out to him and show him that you care about the trials he is facing. Let him know you are there when the periods of fear, anxiety and loneliness come along. Go for walks with him and try and be a listening friend. In times of great pain it can be the things we don't say that are most important.

Counseling the Camper from the Inner City

Having campers from the inner city can be an exciting experience for you as a camp counselor. Most children who live in urban communities never see the beauty of forests, lakes and mountains. Everything they see and experience is a new thrill and life is an adventure of new discoveries. Urban campers are those who come from the inner-city neighborhoods. The word "urban" may conjure up all kinds of images to you but in this context we are referring to the downtown or other highly-impacted communities in our cities.

The Camper

These campers are forced to live life in a different manner than most suburban youth. They will have the same dreams and hopes for the future as any other camper, but their current circumstances will play a heavier role in their lives. If you see the urban community as a distinct subculture you will begin to understand the principles involved in ministering to those kids. In some cases urban campers will have a different vocabulary, a distinct manner of dress and an unfamiliar set of values. Don't expect them to come to camp and immediately assume the role of the average suburban camper.

His Needs

If you have a group of inner-city campers they will probably prefer to stick together in their activities. This gang image is their system of protection and security. In many urban settings youth never travel more than a few blocks from their own neighborhood due to the safety their neighborhood provides. At camp that safety is gone and it may take a few days for a sense of security to return. Their gang represents nothing more than their attempt to maintain group belonging and security.

Inner-city youth are familiar with a great deal of personal freedom. Their parents may not watch them closely. In some cases they may be living with friends or relatives. Because of the frequent lack of a parent in the family, the youth are often forced to take care of the children while the adults are at work. These youth are forced to take on adult responsibilities at an early age in order to care for the needs of their brothers and sisters. This results in a great degree of freedom for them at an early age.

Try and understand that the inner-city camper will have come from an environment drastically different from the camp. And any time a person makes a major change there will be feelings of insecurity and apprehension. Seek to alleviate those feelings as soon as possible but don't expect an overnight transformation.

How You Can Help

Ministry to the urban campers begins by developing a trusting relationship with them. They are leary of establishing new relationships at first but as the week progresses, you should be able to make inroads to their life. As with any different culture, seek full understanding before you make any value judgments.

Ministry to these campers may simply be a matter of gaining their respect and trust. This can be done over a period of days as you play sports with them or teach them a new skill or craft. Since they are excited by their new environment use it as an opportunity to take them on hikes, go exploring together—have fun. As you do this you will be building bridges for a relationship to develop.

If the camper starts off by misbehaving, try and understand the cause of the behavior. Are they trying to get additional attention or to test you? If you establish a system of rules be sure it takes into account the camper's lack of previous restrictions. Be sure he understands the rules of the camp first. Be firm in your discipline but not overbearing. Above all, be fair and don't show partiality between urban youth and campers from other backgrounds.

When you have campers in your cabin from multi-ethnic backgrounds, don't lead with an attitude of superiority. Realize that you can learn some things from them too. Don't forget that in God's eyes all men have equal standing before His throne. Christians are brothers and sisters in the same family. Don't allow campers to demonstrate their prejudicial attitudes at camp. Let them see by your example that all men and women are equal in God's eyes as His Children.

Counseling the Camper Who Has Been Abused

It is unfortunate that abuse in all forms has become so widespread in our society. Due to the number of children who are abused each day in our cities, it will not be uncommon for you to have one or more abused campers in your cabin. When this occurs you will have the opportunity to minister to someone in great need. You can have a life-changing effect on the camper who has been abused.

It has been estimated that over one million children are abused each year in America. Of those children 2,000 will die as a result of the abuse they receive. That is an alarming number of children! It is no wonder that many camps have these children in their programs each year. The Christian camp can reach out to these needy young people with the message of hope and understanding. Abused children will present the counselor with a unique challenge. How do you detect child abuse? How can it be confirmed? Who should you tell if you suspect one of your campers has been abused? What can you do as a camp counselor in just one week with an abused child? These questions and many more are but a few of the issues you will have to face as you minister to abused children.

The abused child may not indicate his abuse to you. You must first detect it by the way he acts. He may refuse to undress for a shower with other campers around, they may turn down invitations to go swimming—all as an attempt to hide the evidence of their abuse. Of course many campers who have not been abused will act in the same manner, particularly young campers who are embarrassed by their changing bodies. Be careful not to jump to conclusions. Simply keep these things in the back of your mind.

There are actually two kinds of abuse that your campers may have received. The first is physical abuse such as beatings, batterings, etc. This type of abuse is easier to recognize and detect. The second type of abuse is sexual molestation. This abuse is very difficult to see but will leave emotional and spiritual scars which will take much longer to heal. Both types of abuse will appear so ministry to both will be discussed in this section.

Ministry to the Physically Abused

If one of your campers comes to camp with a number of scars, burns or cuts on his body, he may be the recipient of abuse. Ask gentle yet persistent questions about them. If the camper received those bruises during the course of a sports activity, he will probably volunteer the information with pride, for those scrapes and cuts are his badge of bravery. If, however, he is very hesitant to discuss them with you, try other approaches. Many times the camper who has been abused will not hide the scars but will make other excuses for them. Try and reconcile the reasons given and see if they seem possible. For example, a camper with a split lip, a black eye and bruises on his back may tell you he slid into home plate during a baseball game.

If you suspect physical abuse with one of your campers you may also notice that he flinches when you put your hand on his shoulder. Does he overreact to you when you come near him? Perhaps he is very aggressive himself with other campers. Either of these behaviors may support your observations.

If you counsel with a camper who admits he is a victim of child abuse, you will need to speak with the camp director. Many states and provinces require by law that all cases of child abuse be reported to the local police department. Some states require notification even if the abuse is just suspected. In any case it is the camp director who should make such a call.

If you suggest that a camper has been battered you should take the following steps: First, set in motion the process of long-term care by contacting local authorities. A call should be made to a child protection agency, a police or social services agency. That will begin the process of protecting the child from further harm. These experienced professionals work closely with the child's school to ensure the harassment and physical abuse is stopped. They will not directly contact the parents until positive evidence confirms the abuse. Until that time they will monitor the child at school. The welfare of the child is the highest priority.

Second, realize your limitations. You cannot change the home nor can you make a lasting change on the camper. Your ministry with that child is a divine opportunity to reassure him that love does exist in the world.

Third, develop a level of trust with the camper. Take him on hikes, go swimming and play games together, etc. Through these activities you will be establishing a base for further communication. Help him realize that the abuse he has been receiving is not his fault. Many times a parent will make the child feel as though he is getting what he deserves. No child *ever* deserves that kind of treatment. Calm his fears and help him realize that God is concerned about his problems and wants to help too.

Fourth, prepare the child for his return home. There will be many fears and apprehensions about this return and whatever you can do to help relieve these anxieties will be of help to him. You can help prepare him by talking to him abut the abuse which he has received. The more he talks at camp the greater the possibility that he will talk to someone else when he returns home. Encourage him to speak with his school counselor, youth pastor, etc. But remember—some kids will want to talk about it, others will not. The latter needs to be encouraged to open up about it to others who can help them.

Last, the camp director should be sure some contact is made with a youth pastor in the camper's neighborhood. Seek to provide the camper with a friend at home with whom he can confide. It is important for the camper to be able to talk about his needs with someone on a regular basis. By helping to build this relationship, you will be doing much to help on a long-term basis.

Ministry to the Sexually Molested

The second kind of child abuse victim you may have in your cabin is the child who has been sexually molested. Recent statistics show this to be a very prominent problem in our communities. It is also a current dilemma in our churches as well and may be one of the best-kept secrets of our Church community. It is far more prevalent than we know, for estimates suggest that only one in four cases are ever reported to a police or social agency.

There are few physical signs of sexual molestation and girls are victims far more frequently than boys. It would not be uncommon for a girl's counselor to have several victims of molestation in her cabin each week so don't be afraid of dealing with campers with this problem.

The profile of such a camper would include the inability to relate to males. They may have an extreme amount of guilt associated with this activity and will have a willingness to accept the blame in some cases. A camper who is trying to reach out for help may make an appointment to talk with her counselor and then break it off at the last minute. This may happen several times. They may also come and talk to you and say, "I have a friend who . . . . " Their approach is often roundabout in order to determine your willingness to discuss this delicate issue.

The procedure for ministering to the sexually molested is similar to that of the camper who has been beaten. First, contact should be made with the camp director. If he has been a director for any length of time he will have dealt with this problem before. He will contact the local authorities and file a report according to the laws of the state or province. This will set in motion the process of long-term help for the child.

Second, realizing your limitations as a counselor, try to initiate the process of forgiveness. The guilt may be deeply ingrained in the camper and in such cases it may take a long period of time before a realization of forgiveness may occur. Often the adult who is molesting the child will make her feel as though she is to blame for the act. In this situation the guilt that is associated will go far deeper than other forms of sin. Begin by reading passages from the Scripture which direct the child toward peace and forgiveness. Reassure the camper that the molestation is not his fault. He will need to be reminded of this many times before it finally sinks into his heart. Don't expect an overnight cure to a long-term problem like this. You can, however, begin the process for them. Underline these verses of Scripture in their Bible so when they go home they can find these reassurances again.

Third, prepare the child for his return home. Understandably, the child will be feeling very anxious so what you do before he goes can aid in the event. Let the camper know that many girls face this problem and that they are not alone. Remind her that it is not her fault and that she is not to blame. Convince her of her worth and value. Reaffirm her self-respect.

Fourth, attempt to contact a person in her neighborhood who can continue the counseling process. Perhaps the wife of a pastor or youth pastor in the neighborhood can assist. A social worker in her community would know of skilled people who can lend help to this camper. Keep in touch with the camper yourself and remind her of your love and concern.

Counseling the Juvenile Delinquent Camper

The period of adolescence is a time of great transition and change. Significant events are happening in a youth's physical, emotional, social, mental and spiritual development. It is not an easy time for youth, their parents or for other adults who associate with them. The counselor must dedicate his life to helping the adolescent negotiate this traumatic period of human development. It is no wonder that many adolescents wander off the road of normal behavior during their travels in life. Many of them will return to the road of normality in time, but for some the detour amounts to a long and difficult course of events. As the counselor of a juvenile delinquent camper, you will have the opportunity to direct the youth back to the right direction of growth and development, but it will not be easy.

The Camper

Several characteristics will comprise the profile of this camper. He may have any combination of the following list:

1. Impulsive behavior
2. A high reliance on peers
3. Lack of personal direction in life
4. Family abnormalities
5. Lower than average physical health
6. Depression
7. Low self-esteem
8. Lack of personal discipline
9. Difficulty relating to adults
10. School difficulties.

Many of these characteristics will be seen in the life of juvenile delinquents. They are closely related to each other and when one element is resolved, it opens the door for further progress to be made in other areas.

His Needs

The juvenile delinquent needs positive camp family relationships, for he is closely tied to his home environment. And although value formation takes place largely in the home first, they also need positive peer influence. As they grow older the influence that their peers have on them grows. This is illustrated in the following chart:[1]

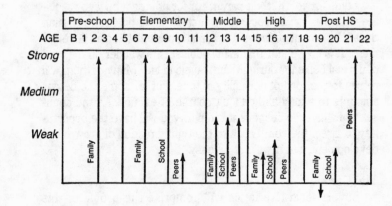

The delinquent youth also needs to have his self-esteem improved. He needs to see himself as a person of value and worth. His behavior must be channeled toward activities that will help build his self-respect. He needs positive role models and consistent standards of conduct.

How You Can Help

Ministry to campers who are juvenile delinquents must be directed to a positive role model. They need firm leadership and need to see this leadership demonstrated. Your standards of judgment and value system should stand the test of time and reality. If they seek a weak leader they will lose their respect for you altogether.

You will need to get them involved in an experience charged with positive peer influence. Let them experience what good friends can be like on a small scale. You can do this by taking them on a hike with one or two other campers who are also leaders. Take them canoeing and swimming with other campers. Try and use teachable moments to point out the benefits of positive peer relations.

Spend time talking to them about their future plans in life. Most of them will not have any since they live so impulsively. They need to understand that their future hopes and dreams (family, job, security, etc.) depend largely on their present life-style. Help them understand the relationship between the two. Encourage them to verbalize and formulate their goals for the future—perhaps for the first time. Also have them make some plans on a small scale so they can see the positive benefit to proper behavior. At the beginning of their week have them write down all of the activities they would like to participate in at camp. As you go through the week, evaluate the kind of progress you are making with them. The discipline it takes to get everything accomplished in a week will be the same as what is needed in life as a whole.

Don't focus your attention on their deviant behavior. It may only be a symptom of a greater need such as attention, love, understanding, etc. As you help meet these needs in constructive ways you may find that the deviant behavior decreases as well. In most cases the deviant behavior is the campers' attempt to get others to notice them. If they can get this attention without the misbehavior while at camp, then perhaps it can work for them at home as well. Help the camper to realize the relationship between their needs and their behavior.

There is a good chance that you can have a significant impact in the life of a juvenile delinquent camper in the short week at camp that you share together. Don't expect to see a complete transformation. In most cases the deviant behavior is a result of many years of reinforcement. Your week at camp together can be a turning point for him. And only in rare cases will you be able to make any significant impact on the hard core delinquent. The strong-willed delinquent may need long-term help which cannot be attained in a week at camp. Do the best you can in those cases and don't feel like a failure if you do not see lasting results. You may be planting the seeds of change by your friendship; seeds that will take time to grow after the camper has returned home. Many long-term problems take long-term solutions.

Questions for Further Discussion

1. What kind of contemporary issue will you have the greatest difficulty handling? Why?
2. What will you do when that issue is seen in one or more of your campers?
3. How can you encourage the camper who is at camp while their parents split up? What can you do to take his mind off the problem?
4. Are there any ethnic groups that you will have difficulty accepting as campers in your cabin? How will you respond if you have campers from this group in your cabin?
5. What will you say if you enter your cabin and find several of your campers arguing with other campers from a different ethnic background? What Scripture will you use?
6. What activities or behaviors will make you suspect that one of your campers has been abused? What will you say or do to confirm your suspicion?
7. What will you say to one of your campers when she tells you that she has been sexually molested? What is the procedure for helping her?
8. Why is sexual molestation such a difficult form of abuse to detect? How will you know if one of your campers has been molested?
9. How will you minister to a camper who has been sexually molested in the past or is currently being molested? What Scripture will you share with this camper?
10. What forms of deviant behavior can you expect to see at camp? How will you respond to them?
11. At what point should a juvenile delinquent be sent home? What can you hope to see happen in the course of a week?
12. What will you be doing to prepare for ministering to a camper with one of these contemporary issues in their life?

9
The Counselor
Training Program

Counselor preparation involves time and effort on the part of the camp or church, but it will help to ensure a successful camp. Counselor selection should be completed well in advance of the camp so that adequate time is available for preparation.

The purpose of any camp counselor training program is: (1) to acquaint the counselor with the philosophy and purpose of that particular camp; (2) to challenge him to the work and ministry of camping and counseling; (3) to reduce any anxiety, feelings of inadequacy and to handle any questions that the counselor may have; (4) to give some basic experience in the area of actual counseling procedures and situations *before* the camp gets under way and (5) to learn how to work with campers.

The training approach should be threefold:

1. Reading in the area of camp counseling and camper characteristics

2. Group discussion with emphasis on personal feelings toward the prospect of counseling

3. Group and individual involvement in roleplaying and analyzing of actual camping situations.

Reading

This book will serve as an essential beginning in the area of reading as a basic background for camp counseling. An extensive bibliography has been included for the purpose of providing other resource materials. Books in the area of children and adolescent characteristics will help to understand the age group. Other books in the area of counseling, camp lore, camp recreation, camp maintenance and camp programming will give a wider exposure to the total program of camping. This will lead to a deeper appreciation for the camp's philosophy and value of other personnel to the total program.

Group Discussion

This will be a supportive and insightful device as counselors seek to alleviate their fears and gain support and understanding of this new ministry—camp counseling. As a group of new or experienced counselors meets together, opportunity for getting to know one another can be provided. Any group needs a feeling of rapport and comradeship before they really function well together as a group. When group members feel comfortable with one another, they feel enough at ease to express their inner feelings. The group discussion situation should be structured in such a way that basic questions about the camp and the work can be aired and discussed. These can be answered, not only by the leader, but also by other group members.

Fears about working with specific age groups, what to do in this or that circumstance, how to cope with a behavior problem, how to get to know my campers and to whom am I responsible: these are just a sampling of some of the questions that will be raised.

Evaluation of Camp Case Studies and Situations

This will be the most valuable training device that a camp and church can use as it projects the counselor into the actual counseling situation with a minimum of danger for "goofs" in the counseling relationship. The cases presented in the book are for the purpose of actual practice and the questions and cases presented can be handled in the following manner: Counselors can react to the questions on an individual basis and attempt to arrive at a solution. The findings can then be shared with the entire group so they can be evaluated. Further analysis can take place at the group level. Roleplaying should be used with these cases as well as other cases and examples that members of the group may contribute.

Roleplaying is simply a method of human involvement or interaction that involves realistic behavior, but in imaginary situations or past experiences. It is a method of reconstructing past situations and viewpoints for analysis and evaluation by working through them in a simulated life manner. Roleplaying is not only a training device for the participants, but an information-giving situation for those in the observation role.

The participants learn by doing and the observers learn by watching, analyzing and identifying. It makes a person self-conscious and thus very aware of his behavior and actions, bringing them into a new focus. He becomes more sensitive to his actions and the underlying feelings. This in turn helps one to develop a greater sensitivity toward others' feelings and problems.

Another value of roleplaying is that it is one of the better methods of improving relationships within groups of people and it allows active participation with real problems. Freedom for experimentation is also available without the danger of making mistakes that are detrimental to the other individual involved. By roleplaying, you have the opportunity to project yourself into the situation of the other person and gain a better understanding of their feelings and attitudes.

As you attempt to set up roleplaying situations, proceed with a case or situation that is familiar and not too threatening. The person leading the group should be warm and friendly and relaxed so the group will respond accordingly. Select those counselors who are secure and confident as the beginning participants will lessen the threat for the others. As you prepare for the actual roleplaying situation, the description of the situation should be explained to all present.

Background information can be given and those who will act out the problem can be selected. The role or character given in a specific case will be given to the prospective counselor and he will then proceed to act out the case or situation. The leader should clarify the fact that roleplaying is different than acting. This is not a test of acting skill. Because the person is going to enact a role, he will need some background or framework out of which to work and proceed. This can be done by the leader giving information, questioning the person as to how he feels he will react and allowing the person to think through his role for a few moments before proceeding with the roleplay.

One person is selected as the "counselor" and one as the "camper." The camper will present the problem as though it is his very own and will talk in the first person. The counselor responds to this person and the roleplaying is in motion. In many roleplaying situations, those involved actually interact according to their own personality structure and the roleplaying becomes real as they become enmeshed in the actual situation.

There are many variations to roleplaying. Some groups will want to deal with the same case several times and as soon as one member has had the opportunity to approach the camper's problem in his way, another may wish to tackle the situation. Perhaps the counselor and camper will switch roles and attempt to see the problem from the other's vantage point and framework. In roleplaying where just two of the members are involved, the rest of the group would profit from some guidelines as there is a maximum of participation on their part. They can be asked to look for voice changes in the participants, body tension or facial expression and gestures, for these express the inner feelings and tensions that are present.

Assumptions and motives can also be observed. Before the observers have an opportunity to comment on what took place, those directly involved should express their own performance and feelings. They may be able to see how they should have reacted or what they should have said and the camper can express how he felt when the counselor was making a specific statement to him. This helps one to see what he is really expressing and how others hear and interpret us.

The others can be given a list of questions to consider as they observe and evaluate. Even a preplanned form can serve as a guide. When the observation group comments, the discussion should be focused on the problem itself rather than on the person.

Others may wish to show their constructive suggestions by demonstrating how they would have handled the situation. In order to draw out the audience or observers, questions such as "What were the reactions to this statement?" or "Was it what was said or how it was said that caused the camper to react in that way?" or "Why did that particular camper's remark bother the counselor so much?" and finally, "What would you have said?" When they desire to tell you what they would have said and done, have them demonstrate.

Much of the value of roleplaying depends upon the discussion and analysis after the session, and this is somewhat dependent upon the observations of the others. All members of a training group should go through the experience of roleplaying and this will take time, perhaps two or three sessions together.

Another approach would be to divide the training group into smaller groups of three. Give each group a typical camp situation, a real case study, or let the members devise their own. One member acts as the counselor, one as the camper and the third as an observer. The camper presents and structures the situation and the counselor attempts to deal with this for about 10-15 minutes.

The session is stopped and the observer presents his view as to what he saw and felt. The camper discusses his own reactions and feelings. Then the roles are reversed with the camper becoming the counselor and the counselor becoming the camper, and the same or a similar process is repeated. The same discussion procedure is followed and then the observer can switch roles with a member.

To further aid the discussion process, two groups of three members each can get together to discuss their experience. Then the entire group can share together. This method will deliver information in a way that no other method can do. It will change and develop attitudes; it will deal with fears and anxieties and help to dispel them. It will also create a more secure counselor and will create awareness on the part of this person. He, in turn, will be more sensitive in his relationships with others.

It would be a good idea to consult with the camp ahead of time about any pre-camp training you do as a church group. Many camps have their own materials and approaches to counselor training. Also, you will want to be aware of camp policies, themes, resources, etc. made available to you. Most camps would be happy to discuss this with you in advance of your arrival.

10

Camper Case Studies

Genuine growth in camp counseling comes only through the process of counseling face-to-face with the camper, encountering him in an honest, interpersonal relationship. However, don't be fearful of realizing your fullest potential as a counselor because of a lack in experience and knowledge. As a counselor, you will develop insight and objectivity as you grow more confident in the camping situation.

Preparing for camp will take hours of involvement. And this isn't work that falls just at the reading level. Seek opportunity to exercise your counseling skills and discuss your feelings of frustration, as well as elation, with other counselors, church personnel or camp leaders.

You need the experience of an actual counseling situation, the confrontation of a major discipline problem, the practice of using the Scripture when leading a person to Christ or leading a cabin group discussion and devotions. This section of the book will attempt to deal with these needs by presenting guidelines and case studies for practice. The cases presented here are true, with the names of individuals and camps changed.

The first step to understanding campers is to understand

yourself. You need insight into your own life—your motivations, fears, feelings, needs, desires, interests and attitudes. In addition, you must learn how to handle these parts of yourself before you are capable of helping others.

Reading the Case Studies

As you read the cases presented here, there are several items to look for and to consider:

(1) Read the case several times. (2) Consider the problem. Identify it or indicate if there is more than one problem. (3) What are the feelings that may be expressed or contained? What do you think are the needs of each person here? Why does he act in that way? (4) How do you feel toward the people in the case? Why do you react toward them in that manner? Whom do you like and dislike? (5) Is there any possible way the problems may have been prevented? (6) How would you deal with the problem? What are the possible solutions and alternatives? What action would you take or whose assistance would you seek? (7) Is this a typical situation that may come up in your camp? (8) What do you think the reaction of the other members of your training group or counseling group will be? Can you see why you attempt to deal with the problem in the manner in which you do? Will your method be successful?

Hopefully, your answers will be discussed, shared and reacted to by the others as insight gathers from involvement with others. This will be of great benefit to all.

Basic Questions in Camp Counseling

1. What are some of the interpersonal problems that may arise between counselors?

2. As you check the beds in your dorm, you find that a camper has a problem with enuresis. You've asked the campers to let you know if this was a problem but there was no response. What are the steps that you would take? Who would you consult and how would you confront the camper?

3. Several members of your dorm are teasing a camper

because of a stuttering and speech impediment. How would you react to those teasing and how would you counsel with the camper?

4. One of the fellows in your dorm is very effeminate. Several remarks have been made about this person by the other fellows and some of the girls. You've even overheard a couple of the other counselors talking about him. Should you attempt to handle the problem yourself or should you seek assistance? If so, to whom will you go? How will you react to the other counselors?

5. On the first day of camp, you've noticed a camper who stands off by himself and appears lonely. How should you approach him and what might be the problem here?

6. One of the girls in camp came running into the chapel and sobbed, "I'm just no good. No one can forgive me for what I did. Can't someone help me, please?" Would you approach this camper immediately with some Scripture? Would you attempt to have a woman counselor talk to her? What would you do with other campers who are there talking to you at that time?

Case Study 1

It was an early August afternoon when, upon returning to his cabin, Chuck noticed most of his junior campers just sitting around, looking for something to do. "Hey guys, why don't we go for a hike up to Misty Falls?" he asked.

"But we didn't think we were allowed to go up there," the campers replied. Chuck told them that it would be fine as long as they didn't tell anyone where they were going. With that the boys jumped up with excitement about the upcoming adventure.

The fellows had a great time sliding down the waterfall and swimming in the lower pool. It was an ideal opportunity for Chuck to be able to spend some time together with his campers and establish relationships with them away from the other campers.

On the way back to camp they decided to take a side trail and hike through the forest. They were having fun hiking and exploring this out-of-bounds area. Suddenly one of the campers stepped on a wasp nest and a dark cloud of wasps engulfed the boys. Many ran screaming into the forest, bumping into trees as they ran. Others stood still and tried in vain to shake them off. Chuck cried out, "Everyone run back to the road—quick!"

When they all got back to the road they discovered that each one of them had been stung several times. At first they laughed at the pain they were all experiencing. It wasn't so bad knowing everyone else was going through the same pain. They still had an hour's worth of hiking left when one of the boys named Ken began to have difficulty breathing. Ken found it hard to walk straight or keep up with the rest of the boys. He looked at some of the places where the wasp had stung him and noticed the areas were badly swollen.

"I don't feel so good, Chuck," he cried. "I feel real sick and I can't breath very well either." At this point Chuck looked at his watch and realized that he was going to be late getting the campers back to camp. Not wanting to show up late and have to answer a number of questions from the dean about where he had been, he told the campers to start jogging back.

Shortly afterwards, Ken collapsed on the road and began to shake violently. "Hey, look at Ken!" the other campers shouted as they looked back up the trail waiting for Ken to catch up. They all ran back to help him and upon arriving at the spot where Ken was lying, some of them began to panic, crying and shouting for help. Some yelled at Chuck, "What are we going to do now?"

Questions

This kind of problem is rather complex. It shows how a simple act of breaking camp rules can suddenly become a major issue. It is not uncommon for counselors who do not understand the reason for camp rules to feel that they can be the exception. Some counselors feel they can gain a special rapport with their campers by breaking some of the camp rules. They feel it makes them look more important in the campers' eyes because they are special. The problem begins, however, when breaking those rules leads to dangerous consequences, particularly for the campers' health and safety. Does the camp you are counseling at have any rules that you need to be aware of like this? If so, are there any that you do not understand? Are there any "out-of-bounds" areas near your camp that you need to be aware of as a counselor? Do you understand the reason for these areas?

How would you have acted after your campers encountered the wasp nest? What could you have done to have prevented getting into such a situation as this? Having encountered the wasps, what other potential dangers could the campers have gotten into? If you were Chuck, what would you have done differently as soon as you got back onto the road with all of your campers? What could Chuck have brought with him in case of such an accident as this? Does your camp have the proper equipment and medical supplies to be prepared for such an emergency? If so, do you know where they are located at your camp? Do you know the correct methods of dealing with a camper who is allergic to stings? Have you ever learned the proper methods of using a bee sting kit? How should Chuck get Ken back to camp? Who should go back for help? Discuss your feelings as if you were: Chuck, Ken or the camp dean.

Case Study 2

The meeting had started and the last of the campers was scurrying to find his place. Two counselors, Janice and Joanne, were standing at the back of the room looking over the group to see if they could assist some in finding a place to sit. The pianist had begun to play and a rousing chorus was being sung with a great deal of enthusiasm.

As the two counselors stayed toward the back of the room, one of the campers came in obviously out of breath, and as she looked for a place to sit down, she noticed the two counselors in the back. She walked up to them and said, "Guess who I just saw walking toward the woods—Carol and Jim. I think they're ditching the meeting. They were sneakish about it, looking back to see if anyone saw them. Boy, wait until I tell the others."

Before she could leave, Janice caught her and said, "Sandy, why don't you let us go and find out what is happening out there and let's not mention this to anyone. I think it would just disturb some of those here in the meeting and we don't really know yet if they're the only ones involved, do we?"

"No, I guess not. I'd sure like to tell someone, but I'll go sit down and wait until I see you later," said Sandy.

The two counselors looked around the room for the counselors of the two campers mentioned. They finally spotted them, but they were seated in the midst of the meeting hall with campers all around them. They decided that it would be better not to cause a commotion by asking them to leave and decided to go looking for the campers themselves. As they left the room, Joanne mentioned to Janice, "I don't see how Mary can put up with that girl in her cabin. She's always up to something and now this. You know with her reputation . . . . "

"Yes," replied Jan, "and Jim's no angel. His counselor mentioned that he's tried to ditch every meeting and makes no response at all during cabin devotions. Remember this morning? Jim's the boy that his counselor asked the other counselors to remember in prayer."

The two counselors hurried toward the wooded area where Carol and Jim were last seen. As they approached the area, they couldn't see the campers anywhere and continued to search the area. As they went down the ravine they rounded the bend and almost stumbled upon the two campers. They scrambled to their feet and looked very surprised and sheepish. Both appeared to be very embarrassed and just stood and looked at the counselors.

Questions

What are some of the implications of what occurred here? What should be done? How should the counselors approach this situation? Would it help to have anyone else involved as they talk together? To what extent should another counselor be involved in a corrective situation with another counselor's camper when the counselor is inaccessible? Would you involve the men's or women's dean in this situation? Should the female counselors have taken a male counselor with them? What are some of the positive factors that could arise from this situation?

Case Study 3

As Jim, the new counselor, came into the cabin, he greeted the high school boys in a friendly manner. Their response was anything but friendly and the best remark was a gruff, "Hi there—are you our counselor?" Despite the cool reception Jim was determined to really get to know these boys and try to lead them to the Lord during this week at camp. He knew that these were the fellows who didn't attend church and had come to camp because of their girl friends. Their reason for being at camp was definitely not for the spiritual rewards!

As Jim moved from fellow to fellow asking their names and shaking hands, he noticed that most of them were sharp, clean looking young men. It wasn't long before one of the fellows turned to the counselor and said with a grin, "Hey, I heard this was the type of camp that tried to convert ya. Man, are they going to have a job gettin' me to be religious!" At this, all the other fellows hooted and laughed. The boys in the cabin started to talk among themselves and seemed to ignore Jim.

Every now and then as Jim straightened his bunk and belongings, he heard a number of four-letter words and the profanity from the fellows increased the more they talked. Occasionally, one of them would look over toward him working at his bunk to see what type of reaction was coming. The language continued and seemed to be a natural part of the conversation.

As Jim continued to work at his bunk the language deteriorated rapidly into real vulgarity. In fact, it was now so loud and noticeable that Jim was sure the campers and counselors in the other cabins could hear.

Questions

What is really happening here? What is this behavior expressing? What are some other ways that campers can test a counselor? What fears and anxieties do you think Jim has because of being a new counselor? How might he react because of a lack of experience? How serious is this language problem? Although this is the normal speech pattern for these boys, how would you attempt to approach them about this? Would you ask for assistance with this problem? Would you handle this differently with junior high and junior campers? If so, how? How important is the initial handling of this situation? Should this problem be ignored to see if it might go away or must every problem be tackled in the initial stages so it doesn't get out of hand?

Case Study 4

The evening was warm and the junior boys in the cabin were restless even though they had been active all day. Ken, their counselor, was sure they would drop right off to sleep because of the day's activities. The devotions had gone particularly well this evening with several of the boys participating and sharing. Even the more reserved fellows prayed tonight.

The lights had been out for about five minutes and from time to time Ken heard a few snickers from the other side of the dorm, and the rustling of paper. He let this slide by for about 10 more minutes and then said, "OK guys, it's late and we want everyone to knock off the noise and go to sleep, OK? We've got a big day tomorrow." The noise diminished and Ken settled down for some rest, but in a couple of minutes several of the boys burst out laughing and in no time every boy in the room was contributing to the uproar.

Ken was out of bed in an instant and switched on the light saying, "That's about enough out of all of you. The next boy that makes a sound is really going to get it. Now be quiet!" The silence was deafening. Not a peep came out of any of them. Ken stood there for a minute, said, "Thank you," turned out the light and went back to bed.

The silence lasted almost until he was settled and then someone snickered and the entire dorm exploded in laughter. Again, Ken hopped out of bed and switched on the light.

Questions

Do you think this is a spontaneous situation or could the boys have planned something like this together? Would this make any difference as to how you would handle the problem? What is the best way to handle a problem such as this? Was Ken correct in his approach? Which of the following actions would have been a helpful next step?

1. Threaten to take the instigating boy or boys to the camp dean or director.

2. Have the boy who instigated the action stand outside for five minutes.

3. Have those involved do 20 push-ups to let them know that you want them to fall asleep. This would help to tire them out even more.

4. Ask the boys as a group what they think they should do and have them discuss the possibilities and consequences.

Case Study 5

Linda's cabin of junior girls had been very well behaved all week at camp. They spent a great deal of effort making sure their cabin was one of the cleanest in camp each week. They received the "cleanest cabin of the week" award and had been quiet during each afternoon rest period. They had also been very diligent in memorizing their Scripture verses and had not been involved in any cabin bickering. Linda was so pleased with her cabin of girls that she wanted to do something extra special for them before they returned home on Saturday. Linda decided to take her girls for a hike to the end of the meadow for a swim in the warm pools that formed in the creek nearby.

The meadow was quite a distance so they set off right after lunch. Linda made sure that the camp director knew where she was going and when she would return. She also took a pack with some cookies and pop for the girls. The afternoon went by much too quickly for the girls as they played in the warm water which ran down the rock slide. Soon Linda realized that it was getting late and that they would need to return quickly in order to get back to camp in time for dinner. They had left a bit too late but they were having so much fun and Linda wanted to give them as much time at the pool as possible.

As they headed back Linda remember a shortcut that she

had taken many years ago as a camper herself. She wasn't positive but was pretty sure of the way. Soon she found the right rock that was used as a marker for the turnoff and she made the turn into the woods. The trail looked pretty much the same even after so many years.

"Stay close girls, we don't want to lose anyone out here," she shouted. It began to get darker as the sun had set a half hour ago. In the forest the shadows grew longer and the light seemed to fade rapidly. The girls were holding each others' hands by now as they stumbled over tree roots and stones in the path. Once or twice Linda would stop and trace her steps back to be sure she was on the right trail. It was getting pretty hard to see the trail now since the sun had set and she was having difficulty remembering the right turns and markers. Suddenly Linda came to a spot in the trail which she recognized as a place they had been an hour before. They had been walking in circles! There was no doubt about it now—Linda's fears had come true as she told the girls they were lost.

Linda began to cry as she realized her mistake. The campers saw Linda's response and began to cry also. Within minutes the forest was awake with the sound of eight girls, sitting at the base of a large pine tree, crying and screaming into the darkness for help. "Somebody needs to go for help," cried Linda. But knowing that she shouldn't leave the girls alone, they proceeded to hike through the forest hoping to find the right way back to camp. It was not long before the campers began to get cold walking in their wet clothes and they began to shiver.

"What are we going to do, Linda?" cried one of the girls.

"I'm cold," cried Terri.

"So am I," whimpered Judy.

As the girls continued to walk through the forest in the darkness, several began to have trouble walking straight. A few of the girls found themselves shivering so much they had trouble speaking clearly. They had slurred speech and could hardly stand. Knowing that the girls would warm up as they walked, Linda encouraged them to walk faster. She had hoped this would generate more body heat. But in a few minutes one of the girls dropped to the ground in a semi-conscious state.

Questions

What should Linda have done before leaving camp to prepare for such a possible problem? What could she have done at the pool to prevent this type of accident from occurring? Was the shortcut really such a bad idea? When would it have been OK for her to have taken the shortcut? What would you have done differently if you were Linda and had just realized you were lost? What were her options at that point? What health problems were the campers facing? Do you know what you would have done had you seen the girls begin to show signs of hypothermia? What three factors can contribute to a camper coming down with hypothermia? This type of problem is not uncommon at camp so don't be misled into thinking it couldn't happen at your camp simply because it is a fine location. Do you know the symptoms and the correct procedure for aiding such a camper? What other supplies should Linda have put into her pack?

Case Study 6

The two counselors walked slowly up the hill toward their cabins, talking about the evening. "That was a message that really got through to some of those girls tonight. I sure wish more of the fellows would respond like that," said Dan. Before Ron, the camp's senior counselor, could reply, seven boys descended upon them talking excitedly and obviously upset. So many were talking that no one could understand a word and Ron had to almost yell before he could be heard. The boys finally calmed down and one of them proceeded to tell what had happened.

"Wait until you see the cabin. Oh boy, were we hit hard. We walked into our dorm and it was a mess. It's terrible!"

Dan asked, "Well, what's wrong with it? What happened?"

The boy who was talking continued, "Someone raided the dorm and we think we know who it was. There's shaving cream all over the bunks, the mattresses are on the floor and the sleeping bags are in the rafters. They dumped our suitcases and I bet there's stuff missing. You just wait and see! There's also pinecones all over the place. We're going to go over to Dorm 8 'cause they did it and, boy, are we going to take care of them."

Ron and Dan both started to talk now. "Now let's wait before you go running off without being sure about the whole situation." Dan had worked with this same group of boys for about three years now. He had been their counselor when they first came to camp in the eighth grade. He knew each boy quiet well, including their strengths and weaknesses. He remembered other occasions when they reacted emotionally first and thought later. In fact, one year one of the boys had been sent home because he was uncontrollable.

At this point Ron assumed control of the situation and started to question the boys specifically about the state of affairs. "Now, why are you so sure that the guys in Dorm 8 did this? Did any of you see them?"

Brian, who had spoken up before, replied, "We didn't have to see them do it. They've been threatening us all week with this dorm raid and now they've gone ahead and done it. Then they had to steal stuff!" All the fellows chimed in at this point and it was a couple of minutes before they were calm enough to proceed.

The questioning continued for a while. Gradually the boys were led to the place where they were ready to return to their cabin with the counselors to survey the damage and actually determine the extent of the missing articles. When they approached the cabin, four of the fellows from Dorm 8 came out and sat on their steps grinning and just watching. As the boys approached their own cabin they slowed down, stared over at the other cabin and stopped.

Questions

This situation is fairly common in most camps and a number of avenues of approach have been selected and listed below. Discuss each and speculate about the possible outcome of each method, indicating strengths and weaknesses:

1. Dan took his boys in the cabin and Ron went over to the boys in Dorm 8 to question them.

2. The boys and the counselors surveyed the cabin. Then they called the camp director to the dorm to give him a firsthand

report and to seek his advice.

3. The boys from Dorm 8 were called over by Dan and asked to step into the cabin with everyone else to survey the damage.

4. All the boys in Cabin 8 were brought together in their own cabin and told that they had been identified as the boys responsible for the dorm raid. Everyone would wait right there until the guilty ones confessed.

5. After surveying the damage, the camp director asked all of the boys in the camp to meet together. During this time, he explained what had happened and asked if anyone had any information concerning the raid. After this, he stated that he would be in his office for the next hour and he would like to have those responsible come to him on their own and discuss what had happened with him.

6. State how you would have handled this problem. How would you have approached the boys in Cabin 8? Would you have approached their counselor or the camp director? How would you have controlled their boys so a fight didn't develop?

Case Study 7

Bruce had been having a challenging week trying to counsel the seven junior high campers in his cabin. They began the week with a negative attitude toward most of the activities and all of the meetings. At first Bruce felt he would never be able to get through to these guys. The campers traveled around camp in a gang which made it difficult for Bruce to establish a friendship with any of them. As the week progressed Bruce was able to slowly work his way into their group and become accepted by them. He did this by not judging them for their different value system and remaining loyal to them. At times it seemed as though Bruce was making some serious progress in leading several of them to the Lord.

Bruce had spoken about his campers at the counselor prayer meetings each morning so the other counselors were praying for them on a regular basis. They had become noticeable by now in the camp and the other counselors were anxious to see these young adolescents make a commitment for Christ. Soon the camp would be over so Bruce decided to make a final appeal to each of them on a one-to-one basis if he could get them apart.

While he sat on his bunk trying to figure out how he would be able to meet with them individually for awhile, one of the campers came in and sat down on his bunk. The camper was a bit surprised to see Bruce in the cabin and it seemed as though he did not really want to have Bruce around. Something else was on his mind. Although Bruce tried to start up a conversation with this camper it was to no avail. When Bruce wasn't looking the camper dug down into his suitcase and snuck a small package into his pocket. Bruce caught the movement out of the corner of his eye and confronted the camper about the package.

The young camper confessed that he had been smoking cigarettes with the other guys in the woods when no one else was around. "All of the other guys do it too," replied the young student. "If you turn me in to the camp director and get me thrown out, you'll have to turn in all of the other guys too!" At that point the camper ran out of the cabin to go and find his other friends. Soon they would be returning to the cabin to speak with Bruce about what he was going to do.

Questions

Bruce has to make a decision about what he is going to do. What are his options as you see them? Discuss the implications of each action he can take. Is it worth turning them in to the camp director so late in the week? Should Bruce overlook the incident in hopes that he will further gain their respect and perhaps be able to win them to the Lord? What would you do at this point? Let's assume the other guys have returned to the cabin. They are all seated around you on the lower bunks. You have their full attention. What will you say to them now?

Case Study 8

Mary was a quiet camper. She appeared to be a very sweet and introspective person and was well liked by her dorm mates. However, her counselor, Rhoda, was concerned because of the apparent lack of response on Mary's part to the Bible study and challenges presented at the evening "Victory Circle" meeting.

On Thursday morning, Rhoda came in a bit late to the general meeting. As she scanned the group of 200 campers, she was able to locate all of hers except one—Mary. She quickly and quietly asked another counselor if she had seen Mary and the reply was negative. Rhoda slipped away from the meeting and went to the dorm and rest rooms to see if she could locate her camper, but she was nowhere to be found.

By this time, Rhoda was worried as this was so unlike Mary.

On the way back to the hall, she stopped at the small prayer chapel and noticed someone sitting quietly in the front row. She recognized and approached Mary. "Mary, I've been looking all over for you. I noticed you weren't in the Bible study and searched all over camp. Is anything the matter?" asked Rhoda.

"Not really," said Mary, "I've been listening to the Bible study and the speaker all weekend, well . . . it's been very helpful and each time he seems to explain how a person becomes a Christian. But I'm not a Christian and I've done some things that have been wrong. Each night I see lots of kids get up and come forward and then come here to the Prayer Chapel to talk with the counselors. Believe me, each night I've wanted to get up and walk forward to become a Christian, but I just didn't have the nerve. I was scared. I want to be a Christian and I want to talk with you alone—not with all the others in here. Will you help me become a Christian now?"

Questions

Is this a common occurrence that would confront you at camp? How might the counselor have worked with Mary before so she would have known about her desire to accept Christ? Indicate the Scriptures and the procedure that you would use to lead Mary or anyone else to Christ. What other procedures would you suggest for a camp to use so campers like Mary would feel more free to indicate their response and make a decision? Because Mary is basically a shy person, how would you counsel her concerning her witnessing as a Christian? Would you help to provide an opportunity at camp for witnessing?

Case Study 9

Steve is one of the most popular counselors at camp. All of the campers seem to like his fun-loving spirit. He never seems to say anything bad about anyone and he always has a smile on his face. He is young and good-looking. It is no wonder that all of the young girls have a crush on him. Steve is quite athletic and enjoys all kinds of water sports. Water skiing and swimming are his favorites. The campers love to watch Steve ski because he is so good and he always sprays the girls standing on the dock as he comes back to shore.

One afternoon down at the lake the campers are watching the ski boat drive by with one of the campers behind it. They are a bit scared about their first attempt and somewhat hesitant to learn. The line, however, is long with anxious skiers. As the other campers watch the boat and the beginning skiers, Steve comes down to the dock with his own personal skis. All of the girls point to Steve as he arrives and look forward to the upcoming show. A crowd begins to form and the campers gather around the skiing area.

Just then Steve waves to his friend who is driving the ski boat, signaling for a ride. The driver enjoys taking Steve because he never falls. The driver spots Steve on the beach and stops to let the skier climb back into the boat. His turn just ended. The driver speeds up and does an impressive turn as he arrives back at the beach.

As the boat arrives Steve gets ready to catch the ski rope from the driver. He is going to do a step start off of the beach to impress everyone with his skiing abilities. But just as the rope is thrown to shore a young camper reaches out and catches it.

"Hey, this is my turn," yells a young boy at the front of the line. "I've been waiting for over an hour for a ride. Why do you get to come down here and just cut in?"

Steve is obviously put out by this young fellow and demands that the ski rope by given to him. The boat driver yells at the camper to hurry up. By now the girls on the beach are yelling at the camper to give up his turn to Steve.

"After all," one of them cries, "you can't ski anyway!"

The other girls begin to laugh at him now. But the camper isn't going to give up his turn. Steve is getting embarrassed and the ski boat driver is getting impatient.

Questions

Assume you are a fellow counselor. What would you do if you were on the beach? How do you think the other campers in line feel about now? Why? What should Steve do now? Why? What would happen if Steve just grabbed the rope and took off with the ski boat? How would the young camper feel? If you are with a group of other counselors at a training session, have a different counselor roleplay each part. Let one of you play the part of the camp director watching this develop from his office up on the hill. After you have played this out, have each person share his feelings about the situation. What could be done to avoid this happening at your camp?

Case Study 10

Richard is an energetic junior high camper. He has come from the County Youth Authority Boys Home with the hope that he will make some kind of decision that will help him get back on the right track in life. The director of the boys' home is very understanding about the type of program that the camp offers and has seen a number of boys make life-changing decisions at camp. Many became better citizens in their community and left their former life-styles behind. It is the intention of the director that camp will have the same effect on Richard.

Glen is Richard's counselor. Glen plays football in college and has a keen interest in working with young juvenile delinquents. He is hoping to get a job as a social worker after graduation from his college in a few years. Glen sees Richard as an opportunity to see what it is going to be like to work with these youth on a regular basis.

Within the first few hours of camp, however, Richard has picked a fight with another young camper. He has also been sent up from the lake by the lifeguard because of disruptive behavior. This is going to be a long week for the camp staff. Already everyone knows about that special camper from "the Home."

On the second day of camp Richard is caught stealing at the snack shack. He is punished by the camp dean by being made to pick up paper around the camp during the afternoon free time. Richard just can't understand why he isn't allowed to go swimming down at the lake with all of the other campers.

On the third day of camp Richard gets into another fight, this time with a junior counselor. Then in the morning meeting Richard disrupts the speaker by telling jokes with the other young boys around him. He is clearly becoming a problem. Each time Richard gets into trouble Glen is sure to sit down with him and explain the details of the crime—also the rationale for the punishment.

By midweek Richard has been caught raiding another cabin and causing a fight between his cabin and the one he raided. He was definitely a leader, but a poor influence. On several occasions Glen has caught Richard smoking back behind the maintenance shed after the evening meetings. It is obvious to Glen since Richard's clothes smell so strong of cigarette smoke when he comes back to the cabin at night.

On Thursday afternoon Richard tips another canoe over in the lake causing several of the campers to have to swim back to shore and abandon their canoe. Richard thinks it is pretty funny since the couple in the other canoe seemed to be getting pretty friendly with each other while nobody was looking. The lifeguard who has to go and rescue the canoe and the two campers doesn't find it very funny though.

It is Thursday evening and the counselors are having their daily meeting while the campers are busy playing a field game. In just a few short days Richard has gotten in several fights, has been caught stealing, has disrupted the morning meeting, has been caught smoking several times, has nearly drowned several campers and has been using foul language. Lately, however, he *has* been paying attention at the meetings.

Questions

You are the camp program director. What are you going to do about the situation with Richard? What are your options?

Assume you are Glen and discuss your options also. What kinds of suggestions would you give Glen if you were a fellow counselor with him that week? Try roleplaying this situation with a few other friends who will be counselors. Outline all of the reasons why Richard should be allowed to stay at the camp. Also discuss all of the reasons why he should be sent back to the boys' home. What are Richard's real needs? How can a counselor minister to them given the limitations of a camp setting?

Case Study 11

It had been a good week for Bonnie since all of the girls in her cabin seemed to get along well together. The only real challenge she had was with Cheryl. She was a shy little girl who never seemed to get involved with the other girls during the camp games and activities. When Bonnie asked Cheryl what was wrong she only got a simple "Nothing," and a shrug of the shoulders. Bonnie didn't want to pry into Cheryl's personal life preferring to wait for Cheryl to express her feelings when the time was just right.

One afternoon the camp director gave out all of the mail. Cheryl received a letter from home but was hesitant to open it. She went off by herself and opened the letter carefully. As she did tears came to her eyes as she read the contents of the letter. Her parents had decided to get a divorce and had picked that week to split up. The letter was to inform her that her mother would be picking her up after the camp was over. Her father would have moved out of the house by then and would be living in another city nearby. Cheryl began to cry uncontrollably as Bonnie came toward her.

Questions

What kind of feelings does Cheryl have right now? What are her fears? If you were Bonnie, what would you do right now? What kind of counsel would you offer Cheryl at this time? What kinds of behavior might you expect from Cheryl in the next few days? What will you and the other girls in the cabin do to help Cheryl get through the remaining days of camp? Have the other counselors in your training group share their feelings about their parents' divorce if any of them went through it as a youngster.

Case Study 12

John was worried when he got out of his bed on the third morning of camp. He was certain that he had heard one of his junior campers crying during the night but he didn't know who it was. It was difficult to tell during the black of night and he hesitated disturbing the others in an attempt to find out. Now most of the boys were awake and actively preparing for the day's events. He thought to himself, *Well, this would be a rather poor time to attempt to find the boy. I'll just have to wait or perhaps the problem will solve itself.* He hadn't noticed any of his campers staying to himself or withdrawing. All of them were actively engaged in the meetings, sports programs and craft activities. Perhaps someone had said something to one of the boys and he was brooding over that, or perhaps he had suffered a disappointment during the day. Whatever it was, John hoped that it would work itself out as he had a strenuous day before him.

It was a full day and everything went well for the counselors and the campers. Following lunch and the foolishness around the table, mail was distributed—an event eagerly anticipated by both campers and counselors. Letters and especially packages of cookies were relished by all. As far as John could tell, letters were received by all of his campers, although he was pretty engrossed in the letter that he had received from his girlfriend back home.

As he left the hall, the camp director approached and asked, "Well, John, how are your campers working out for you? Any problems developing with any of them?"

John said, "Oh no, nothing to speak of anyway. They're a pretty good bunch and they sure participate well."

"Fine. I'm glad to hear that," replied the director. "You've got a couple of eight-year-olds in there and most of the others have never been away from home before except the Roger brothers. If anything arises, don't hesitate to let me know."

"I sure will, and thanks," said John.

The evening passed and the lights went out. About an hour

after the others were asleep, John awoke to hear the sobs of a boy close to him. He arose and almost bumped into Peter. "Hey there, Pete. What's the problem, something wrong?" Pete continued to cry and just shook his head. John guided him firmly outside where they could talk so the others in the cabin wouldn't be awakened. "Come on Pete, what's wrong? I'd like to hear about it," asked John.

The words stumbled out of Pete, and very brokenly, yet firmly, he replied, "Just let me get out of here. I want to go home—and now!"

Questions

What are some of the reasons for homesickness? Do you see any clue in this case that may have given you insight as to the cause? How would you handle this boy and his problem? Should this behavior be expected with this cabin of campers? Why or why not? How can you use preventive measures so this won't occur? In what way would you improve on the way John handled this situation? What positive signs do you find in John's actions?

Case Study 13

Tommy was having a great week at camp. He was learning so many new things. He spent a great deal of his time exploring the creek and playing field games with the other junior campers. It was a most exciting experience for him to be away from home. It seemed as if Tommy just couldn't get enough accomplished in a day.

During the week, his counselor, Mike, noticed Tommy always waiting around until all the other campers had taken their shower before he went in for his. Mike just figured Tommy was shy and really never thought much about it. But as Mike got to thinking about it, Tommy also waited for all the campers to get undressed and into their sleeping bags with the lights out before he would get ready for bed. Mike really never gave it a second thought until one of the other counselors came up to Mike one afternoon and said, "Hey Mike, why doesn't Tommy want to get involved in the water relay games at the pool today? All of the other campers want him to swim in the relay race."

"Maybe he can't swim," Mike said.

"I don't know," said the other counselor, "but I think there might be more to it than that."

Mike decided to seek out Tommy and have a little talk with him.

Mike found Tommy on the hill overlooking the swimming pool. "Hey Tommy, why don't you want to go swimming in the water relays?"

"Oh, I don't know, I guess I just don't want to."

"Can you swim, Tommy?"

"Sure I can, I use to swim on a team at the YMCA during the summers."

Mike began to get somewhat suspicious as he thought through the other circumstances so he began to ask Tommy about his family. Tommy didn't really like living at home. He enjoyed his mother, brothers and sisters but his stepfather didn't get along with him very well. As Mike continued the dialogue he suspected that Tommy's dad may have been pretty harsh on Tommy.

"Does your dad ever hit you, Tommy?"

"Yeah, lots of times." At that Tommy took off his shirt and revealed the scars and burns on his back. Some of the cuts were still fresh and had recent scabs.

Questions

Child abuse is not an uncommon problem among children these days. It is very unfortunate and can be devastating to a young person. It can leave emotional scars that will remain for a lifetime. Imagine that you are Mike in this situation. What would you do? What would you say to Tommy to help him? What are Tommy's feelings, fears, etc. What are Mike's options for getting Tommy some help? What could Mike do or say to prepare Tommy for when he goes home?

Case Study 14

"Boy, am I ever tired of sitting," complained Dick.

"Yeah," laughed Bill. "I counted how long we had to sit there this morning for the three meetings—two hours and 45 minutes. Did you see the schedule that they gave us the first day? Only two meetings in the morning and an hour of athletics. We haven't even been to the athletic field in the morning and now these special seminars or whatever they call them at 4:30! It's gettin' to be too much."

Just then, four other boys came in and one of them asked, "Hey, are you guys with us? We're going to ask Harry about this whole deal of all these meetings. He's counseled here for two years now and I overheard him say he's never been at a camp that's had so much emphasis on meetings. They're cutting us out of two hours of free time."

Their counselor Harry came in and noticed right away that the situation wasn't normal. He looked at a couple of the boys and asked what was going on. The reply was instantaneous. "Harry, what can we do about all these meetings? They told us there would be just so many and that was all right 'cause we know this is a Christian camp. Some of the Bible study they present is good, but we can sit there just so long. They're cutting down on the free time. We're not the only ones who feel this way either. A lot of the girls are griped, too!"

Harry waited a minute before he replied, for he, too, felt as some of them did. The time infraction was actually hampering the program as the campers were becoming restless in the marathon meetings. The messages were lacking in impact because of this factor. He had been bothered about this for the past day and wanted to talk with his camp director, Tom, about the problem. Harry knew, however, before he approached the director, that Tom had encouraged the speakers to take all the time they wanted. If they preferred to have an extra meeting or two, that was fine. The campers were here to learn, first of all, and some of the other activities must take second place when it comes to Bible study. But this put Harry in a rather difficult position because he knew the extra meetings were backed by the director and he had a responsibility to the camp policy. At the same time he had his own reactions to cope with as well as that of the campers.

Harry let his campers continue to talk out their feelings and encouraged them to express themselves by questioning them and helping them to explore not only their feelings, but some of the reasons for the change in programming. Finally, one of them came right out and asked, "OK, Harry, we've told you how we feel. Now, what do you think about this whole problem and what can you do about it for us? Will you go ask the camp director to watch the time and give us back our recreation program?"

Questions

How would you handle a case where your own attitude or opinions are contrary to those of the camp policy? Where does your responsibility lie in such a situation? Are these campers justified in their feelings? Why or why not? Could this problem have been avoided with some preventive methods? If so, how? How should you react when your campers react to the camp program or supervisor? Should you ever agree or disagree? What other course of action is left open for you? Is there ever a time when you should go to those in the place of highest authority in a camp and speak for the campers or recommend a change?

Case Study 15

Rick could see that his small group of campers were deeply engrossed in conversation as they sat around the towering pine tree. As he stood there drinking his Coke, he wandered toward the boys. They were enjoying themselves. Rick really liked this group as they were easygoing and cooperative, and had established a fine relationship from the start. He was well accepted with this group of campers and they were very responsive toward him, eager to have him around and participating.

"Hi, Rick!" a couple of the boys yelled to him as he approached.

"You really look and sound like you're having a ball over here," replied Rick.

"Yeah," said Don, "Frank's telling some great stories. They're out of sight. Go ahead and tell him that last one, Frank. It's great, and the way you tell it really gives it a punch."

Frank looked a little sheepish and said, "Ah, I don't know if he wants to hear it or not. Besides, you've heard it once and I won't get any laughter out of it from anyone else besides Rick. Man, if I'm going to tell a joke, I want an appreciative audience." Most of the boys laughed at this and they encouraged Frank to tell Rick the story.

Rick found a place where he could lean against the tree and Frank began to talk. As the story developed, Rick sensed that the story wasn't the type that he had expected to hear. He was even dubious as the joke progressed from double meanings to out-and-out profanity and vulgarity. The other fellows sat there grinning and enjoying themselves and Frank was very wrapped up in what he was talking about. Frank gave the punch line and once again, the campers roared and howled with laughter and glee. Frank looked over at Rick.

Questions

When smutty stories or dirty jokes are told in the presence of the counselor, what is the best way to react? If this story or joke were told by a junior camper, how would you react? How would you react to a junior higher or high schooler? What type of teaching situations could this lead to and how would you proceed? What would be the advantage of overlooking and ignoring this type of joke? What are the possible results? Is this a situation where you would immediately quote Scripture to the campers and emphasize that "this is a Christian camp and we don't tell those types of stories here"?

Case Study 16

The day had been strenuous for campers and counselors alike and Dave was mighty glad to see his bunk. He had already planned his devotions and they would be brief tonight as his main interest right about now was sleep! By the time "lights out" rolled around, all of the junior high campers assigned to him were ready for bed and ready for devotions.

Dave was a bit disappointed with the response of some of his campers as they were hesitant to enter into the discussion and sharing time that comprised the evening devotional period. But in a way, he was glad that he could finish the devotions in a hurry tonight. And as soon as they finished a round of prayer, Dave settled down to sleep—or so he thought.

"Hey, Dave," he heard someone whisper, "can I ask you a personal question?"

Dave replied, "OK, go ahead."

"You've gone out with girls before. Have you ever kissed any?"

Dave answered, "Well, er . . . yeah, I have a few times. Why do you ask?"

Jim, the boy who had been asking said, "Oh, some of us have been wondering about it. Not so much that you have but what it's like and, oh you know, what you do after that."

By this time, Dave started to suspect that the question Jim was asking was deeper than it first appeared. He could see in the dim light that most of the boys were sitting up waiting for his answer. Finally, Dave answered, "You mean, you guys want to know about sex and what it is?" Several of them replied in the affirmative. Dave went on, "Well, haven't you learned something about this in your science or gym classes at school? And what about your home? Your folks have talked to you about this by now, haven't they?"

The replies varied from, "Naw, not at all," to "Just a little, but I felt funny when my mom started talking about that stuff, so I left."

One fellow in the group named Bob mentioned that his dad came up to him one day and said, "Bob, it's about time that we had a talk about sex and young boys and girls."

"So I said, 'Sure, Dad, what do you want to know?'"

Most of the boys laughed loud and long to this reply until one of the counselors from another cabin adjoining theirs pounded on the wall and yelled something about lights out and time to go to sleep. Dave couldn't help but laugh with the fellows at this reply. Bob went on to say, "Yeah, Dad never said a thing about that again. He came home with a book another time and said I should read it and all that, but I never did."

By now, Dave was wide awake and wondering how he

should proceed. Just then, the counselor from the other side yelled over again and asked them to quiet down. Dave replied to the fellows, "He's right, guys, it's late and we've got to get our sleep."

One of the other boys protested, "But Dave, we want to know about this and we don't seem to have a time during the day. There's always some other guys around or some girls. And if they heard us talking about this, they'd think we were odd or something. I've heard some of the other kids talk about sex but I don't know if what I heard was right or not. What about the Bible? It uses some big words now and then that the minister says has to do with sex, but I don't know what all of them mean. Can't you tell us now?"

Questions
The camp has a time for lights out in the dorms and strives to maintain a set time of rest for the campers. Should Dave continue with the discussion at this time or delay it? What would be the advantages and disadvantages of both methods? Should Dave attempt to handle this or delegate it to someone else on the staff and not discuss it at all? Discuss and adequately explain all of the passages that deal with sex in the Bible and present the biblical view of sex. If you continued the discussion at this time, how would you proceed and how would you deal with the problem of disturbing other campers and counselors who weren't involved in this discussion?

Case Study 17

Cindy became a Christian at the evening camp fire on the third night of camp. She was a nice teenager with a lot of hopes and dreams for the future. She was a friendly girl and was quite popular at camp with other campers her age. Cindy seemed to show signs of spiritual growth even in the few days at camp after she became a Christian. Some of the other girls had commented on the change that they had already seen in her life. That was an encouragement to Shannon, her counselor.

The comments about her changed life caused Cindy to

become worried about what it would be like after she returned home. So, she got together with Shannon in the snack shop for a soft drink. Cindy shared about her background and the details of her family's spiritual values. They were very different from those that were presented at camp. It was because of that difference that Cindy had decided to become a Christian in the first place. Now it had her worried.

After a few minutes of conversation, Shannon concluded that Cindy had come from a home where Jesus was just another good man. They did not believe in His deity or that He would be coming back again. Cindy's family was also involved in a non-Christian group.

Cindy knew that her newfound faith would be challenged by her family. She also believed that she would not last long under the pressure her family would put her through to conform to their beliefs. Cindy wanted to learn as much as she could about the essentials of the Christian faith before she returned home in a few days.

Questions

As Cindy's counselor, what would you do to help Cindy? What areas would you consider to be essential for her to study in the few days that were left in camp? Can you recommend several books that Cindy could get at the camp's bookstore that would help her after she returned home? What passages of Scripture would you share with Cindy and have her underline in her Bible? What could you do to help Cindy after she returned home?

11
Talks for Cabin Devotions

As you begin to put materials together for this important part of your counselor responsibilities, remember the group characteristics of the campers. It would be very helpful for you to review these now before you begin to write your cabin devotions. As you read these camper characteristics, note particularly the mental and spiritual development of the camper. Then, after you have reviewed chapter 4, come back and continue on in this section.

Now that you have reread this important material, you will be able to write devotions that will be more applicable to the needs of the campers you are about to counsel. Try to put yourself in their shoes as you think back on the important issues in your life when you were that age. The concerns you have now will no doubt be very different, so it is important that you put your areas of interest aside, concentrating instead on the issues your campers will be facing when they are at camp.

If you are having difficulty remembering what those interests and concerns were when you were that age, maybe this list will be helpful to you. Remember, there may be some overlap between ages because of the different rates of maturation between boys and girls. Use this material as a general guideline.

Interests and Concerns for Junior Campers:

1. Learning skills necessary for ordinary games and rec-
    reation
2. Building a positive attitude toward their own develop-
    mental growth
3. Learning to get along with others their age
4. Learning an appropriate masculine or feminine social
    role
5. Developing basic skills of reading, writing and concep-
    tualization
6. Developing a conscience
7. Establishing a value system and moral code of conduct.

Interests and Concerns for Junior High Campers:

1. Developing more mature relations with others their
    own age
2. Learning proper attitudes toward authority figures
3. Accepting their physical development
4. Achieving a masculine or feminine social role
5. Developing one's intellectual reasoning abilities
6. Achieving healthy relationships with members of the
    opposite sex
7. Beginning to establish personal independence.

Interests and Concerns for Senior High Campers:

1. Preparing for an occupation
2. Establishing one's independence from parents
3. Preparing for marriage and family life
4. Establishing their own system of values and morals
5. Developing financial stability
6. Developing social skills needed for civic responsibility
7. Achieving socially responsible behavior.

Although this section will give you several devotionals that can be used with your campers, there may be times when you will need to develop your own devotions in order to meet specific needs within your cabin. It is a simple process which, if followed, can be adapted to any age group, interest or concern. It may take a bit of practice but stay with it!

Steps for Writing Your Own Devotional

The first step is to *listen closely to what the camp speaker has said during his morning and/or evening presentation.* It is always a good idea to continue his thought during the cabin devotions you conduct. This can be done by leading into it with questions like, "Before we go to bed tonight, what did the speaker say today that was of interest to you?"

"What stands out to you from the message that was given tonight?"

"Why do you think the speaker used that particular message tonight?"

"What were some of the thoughts you had while the speaker was presenting his talk?"

If you can lead into a discussion from the material that was presented by the camp speaker, you will be building upon a firm foundation in most cases. Because the speaker cannot come to your cabin and ask if there were any questions or comments about his material, you will have to be his spokesman. Perhaps reread the text that he used or review any significant illustrations that were used. Is the speaker using a particular theme that you can support in your cabin devotions?

If this is not a viable alternative for you, proceed directly into the second step by *considering the needs of your campers.* As you have observed them during the course of the day, what areas of concern do you have for them? Do they know the Lord personally? How do they get along with each other? Are there any noticeable problems with the stories and jokes that they tell? If they are Christians already, do they read their Bibles by themselves or do they spend time in prayer? Are they giving of their time to help others? What is their attitude toward the use of money? Do they say critical and hurtful things about others when nobody is around? Do they have habits which they need to break? Do any of them have attitudes which are destructive to their growth and development? What kind of progress are they making on the interests and concerns of other campers their age? These are but a few questions you can ask yourself as you seek to determine their needs.

The third step in the process of writing your own devotions is to *select a Bible story or passage that relates to your campers' interests or concerns.* Consult the lists in chapter 4. Perhaps you can ask the camp dean or program director where you can find material in your Bible related to a specific area of interest. Consult the concordance in the back of your Bible, if you have one, for further helps. Some Bibles also have chain references which give you several related Bible passages to read. Look these up and use for further materials.

Don't feel as though you must prepare a message with three points and a poem for your cabin devotions. Keep it simple! Just read the passage and ask some questions to get the discussion started. You want the campers to talk and discuss together. It is not another time for them to listen to another message. Ask some leading questions by starting your questions with words like, how, why, what, etc. Don't word your questions so they can be answered with a yes or a no. Make them answer with their own feelings and thoughts.

The next step in writing your own devotions is to *wrap up with a significant thought.* You have been letting them talk and discuss the material up to this point. Now let them know that it is your turn. Conclude the lesson by relating a personal illustration or example. Don't try to be real impressive, just be sincere. Say something like, "Up to this point I have heard some interesting ideas from all of you. Let me wrap things up tonight by sharing with you my feelings about this passage of Scripture." Then share a simple illustration or story that will leave them thinking when the light is out and they are lying in their bunks. Have a word of prayer together and ask that the cabin remain silent for the rest of the evening as they go to sleep. It may be fitting later in the week to ask several of the campers to pray. Be careful about doing this with younger campers, however. Ask for volunteers, just to be on the safe side with younger campers.

If, however, you are counseling for the first time or were called in at the last minute and didn't have time to prepare for the first few nights, try using some of the devotionals that are presented in this section. They are written with the interests and needs of each age group in mind. Feel free to adapt the material in any way you like. Make it personal and relate the material to the needs of your campers. Ask lots of questions. If you don't get to the end of the devotional but are still able to have a meaningful discussion with the campers, don't feel as though you need to get through it all in order to have a good cabin devotional with your campers.

Cabin Devotionals
for
Junior Campers

FIRST DAY
THEME: LOST AND FOUND
Read Luke 15:11-24

Have you ever lost something that was very special to you? Perhaps it was a toy or an article of clothing. Maybe you have had a dog or cat missing from home and you had to go and find it. Do you remember how hard you looked for it and how happy you were when you found it? (Allow campers to share about their experiences.)

Try to imagine how much this father loved his son. He loved his son more than anything else in his life so you can be sure that he wanted to get his son back again. He knew his son had to come back on his own though, so all he could do was wait. (God waits for us to come back to Him also.)

The son thought he was going to live such a good life when he left his family but he really didn't know as much as he thought he did. It was a surprise to him to find out how hard it was to live without his friends and family. When he discovered his mistake he did the right thing—he ran home as fast as he could.

His father must have been out in the fields looking for him because when he was still a long way away his father spotted him coming. What does this story tell us about how much this father loved his son? (Illustrate how much God loves each of us even more!)

SECOND DAY
THEME: GIVING EVERYTHING TO GOD
Read John 6:5-13

Jesus felt sorry for the people who had been following Him around the countryside for many days. They had not eaten very much and He was afraid that some of them would get sick without enough food. He wanted to be sure they had eaten a good meal before they returned home so He asked if anybody had any food. Who was it that had the fish and the loaves of bread? How many fish did the little boy have? How many loaves of bread did the little boy have? How much did he give to Jesus?

The little boy gave everything he owned to Jesus. Why do you think he did that? He gave Jesus everything he owned because he knew Jesus could use it. He may not have known what Jesus was going to do with it but he was willing to trust Him. Are you willing to trust Jesus with everything that you own too? At this age you may not own very much and you may be wondering what you could give Him. What do you think Jesus would want from you if He were here now? (Be prepared for some varied answers.) I think Jesus would really only want one thing and that would be your life. If you were willing to give Him that I know He would be willing to give you much more in return, such as forgiveness, peace and permission to come before His Father in prayer. You'll become a child of God by giving Jesus your life. It will cost you everything, but you have everything to gain too.

THIRD DAY
THEME: BENEFITS OF BEING A CHILD OF GOD
Read John 1:12

When I was born into my family I received quite a few things. I received the protection and security I needed in order to live. My parents fed me on a regular basis and cared for all of my basic needs. They did this because they loved me. When I was born into God's family, the day I received Jesus into my heart, I also received some things from my heavenly Father. Actually, I didn't realize how much I received until later. But let me share with you a couple of the most important benefits of being a child of God.

Read Romans 10:9-11. Can anybody tell me what I received when I became a Christian? (You may need to read this passage again but let them figure it out themselves.) That's right, I received my salvation. That's a big word but can anyone tell me what it means? (Let them respond.)

A second item I received when I became a child of God is found in 2 Corinthians 5:17. (Read it now.) What does this passage say that I received? That's right, I was given a new life. All of those bad things I did before are all gone and I can experience hope for a happy future.

One more item I want you to know about is found in Hebrews 5:13. (Read it now.) What does this say I got? (Let them respond.) Yes, I received the assurance that God will always be next to me to help guide me through life. No matter where I am I can know that God is there to help me.

Have you ever become a child of your heavenly Father? Remember how we talked about doing that last night? Can anybody tell me how it is done? All of these benefits and more can be yours when you join God's family too.

FOURTH DAY
THEME: ACCEPTANCE AND FORGIVENESS OF OTHERS
Read Matthew 18:21-35

By this time at camp you have probably noticed that there are a lot of different kinds of campers here with us. Some of them have become your friends but perhaps not all of them. In fact, you may find that there is someone here that you do not like at all; someone that you refuse to play with or join in activities with during the day. Maybe that's also how the disciples felt when they came to Jesus and asked Him those questions.

How do you think the first slave was brought before the king to repay his debt? How happy do you think he was to find out that he didn't have to pay it? What kind of man was the king?

Why do you think the first slave reacted so strongly to his fellow slave? Is it possible that he just forgot how much he had been forgiven? Perhaps he was a very greedy person too!

There will be times in our lives when we will be just like the first slave. Our friends will forgive the bad things we do against them but we won't forgive the bad things they do against us. Jesus told this story because He wanted us to remember that when we became a Christian we were forgiven of a great debt—sin. We must be sure that we are willing to forgive others when they do things to us that we don't like.

FIFTH DAY
THEME: GROWING IN CHRIST
Read 1 Peter 2:2

The verse I just read spoke of the importance of good spiritual food. Have any of you ever seen a newborn baby? What are they like? What do they eat? What would happen if you quit feeding that baby its food? The answer is pretty obvious, isn't it! It wouldn't live very long. In the same way, we as Christians must read God's Word in order to grow strong. Just like newborn babies, we must desire the spiritual food of God's Word.

(Read also James 1:22-24.) James tells us that it isn't enough to just read the Bible but that we must also try to practice what it tells us to do. Imagine how foolish we would all be if we woke up tomorrow morning, got out of our bunks and walked into the dining hall without having changed our clothes or washed up. We would look pretty silly! James tells us that if we read the Bible but don't do what it says, we are just as silly.

It is really important that we read God's Word on a daily basis. It is even more important that we live the life that God describes in His Word. We shouldn't just close up the Bible and forget about what we read. We must be sure that we live out the lessons we learn from the Bible so that we can experience the best possible life. God wants us to read His Word *and* put it into practice. People cannot grow without physical food and Christians cannot grow without spiritual food either.

SIXTH DAY
THEME: PRAYER CHANGES THINGS
Read Mark 1:29-35

Jesus was a very popular man! It seems as though everywhere He went there were people who wanted to meet Him. There were times when Jesus spent all day and all night talking to people and healing those who were sick. It must have been very tiring for Him some days.

The passage of Scripture I just read was a story about just one of those days. From early in the morning until late in the evening, Jesus met with people in need. He must have been very tired when He finally got to sleep. Perhaps it was not until some time after midnight.

Read verse 35 again. What time did Jesus get up the next morning? The Bible doesn't say exactly what time it was but if it was a long time before dawn it must have been around four or five A.M. That means Jesus only got a couple hours of sleep that night. What did He have to do that was so important that He had to get up after only a couple hours of sleep?

We take for granted the fact that we can pray whenever we want. If Jesus felt prayer was so important, maybe we should too! Let's spend a few moments praying together right now before we go to sleep. (Pray with your campers briefly. Perhaps take some prayer requests from them about their concerns when they return home.)

Cabin Devotionals
for
Junior High Campers

FIRST DAY
THEME: ROCKS, ROADS, THORNS AND FRUIT
Read Mark 4:3-8, 13-20

Jesus used a lot of farming illustrations in His teaching. One comparison He made was between people and soil. He said there were four kinds of people on this earth and each could be compared to a type of soil. Let me read the first half of the story and you see which types of soil you can identify. (Read Mark 4:3-8.)

What are the four kinds of soil identified in this passage? That's right. Now listen and see if you can tell me what kind of people each type of soil represents. (Read Mark 4:13-20.) What are the four kinds of people? (Allow them to respond, then summarize their answers.)

Jesus divided all of mankind into these four types of people. There are those who hear about how they can become Christians but ignore it (the hard soil). Then there are those who hear but never make a true commitment (the rocky soil). The third person hears and makes a commitment but as soon as the desires of the world come along, he changes his mind and then the message gets choked out (those among the thorns). The last type of person hears the way to become a Christian, makes a commitment and then sticks it out in life. He becomes fruitful and fulfilled in his life.

As you lie in bed tonight, think about which type of person you are. Ask yourself what you are going to do about the type of soil your life represents. We'll talk more about this later on as we go through the week together.

SECOND DAY
THEME: LIVING LIFE IN THE FAST LANE
Read Luke 15:11-24

Our society puts a lot of emphasis on living life to the fullest. Advertisements tell us to "Go for the gusto," "You deserve the best," "Get all you can out of life," etc. Our culture says that if we want to experience life at its best, we need to have a lot of money, live an independent life-style and live it up. The motto, "Eat, drink and be merry" fits right in.

Let me share with you a story from the Bible about a guy who lived that way long before the television ads were ever around. He lived life in the fast lane. (Read Luke 15:11-24.)

After you read the passage, ask a series of questions to get the discussion started such as:

1. How much money do you think he had? (A lot!)
2. Why did his father give it to him? (He loved him)
3. What city might he have gone to today? (Vegas, New York, Vancouver)
4. What did he do with all of the cash? (Wasted it on his friends)
5. Where were his friends when he ran out of money? (Gone!)
6. What is the worst job you can think of doing?
7. Why did his father take him back? (A lot of love!)

Wrap up the discussion by reminding your campers that many of us have run away from our heavenly Father but that He waits for us to return with open arms. Challenge them to see the futility of living life by our society's standards.

THIRD DAY
THEME: PAYING THE PRICE
Read Mark 15:15-24

All of us want to be the best at what we do. We watch our favorite sports athlete, movie star or musician and dream of being like them. We forget how much effort goes into preparing for being that good.

No matter how hard we try we can never be good enough to get to heaven. God says we would have to have lived a sinless life first. None of us have been able to do that. So, how do we make it? Jesus came and lived a perfect life hundreds of years ago. In doing so, we are now able to get to heaven for eternity. It doesn't cost us very much in comparison to what it cost Him. Let me read to you the story of how much Jesus paid for our salvation. (Read Mark 15:24.)

That was a horrible way to die. It was the most painful way to kill a person at that time. Jesus was beaten severely, ridiculed and spit on by those around Him. He didn't do anything to deserve it, either. Why then, did He go through with it? Simple—for you and for me! He knew that there would come a day when you and I would be born and live here on earth. He also knew that we would fail and make mistakes. The only way for us to get those mistakes forgiven is by asking Him to forgive us. He purchased the price for me to have my sins removed. The price was paid on that cross.

Perhaps some of you need to consider becoming a Christian. Now that you have heard how from the camp speaker, it is time to decide. Let me remind you that it is not a decision to put off.

FOURTH DAY
THEME: MIRROR, MIRROR ON THE WALL
Read Matthew 6:25-34

No matter who you are, you have probably looked in the mirror at some point in time and asked yourself why God made you that way. It is only natural for us to wish we were better in some aspects. Perhaps you have wanted blonde hair instead of brown, blue eyes instead of hazel; maybe you have wanted to be taller or smaller than you are now.

Well, don't feel alone. The disciples must have been feeling the same way too because Jesus gave them something to think about one day. (Read the passage.)

Evidently the disciples wanted to be sure that their life would be planned out neatly. They may have also wanted to have better-looking clothes, to have been a little taller than their friends or to have all the food they could eat. Yes, even Jesus' disciples were worried about the future.

But Jesus gave them some good advice. He gives us the same advice too. Don't try to live tomorrow's events today. Concentrate on today's activities. Sure, there are times when we need to prepare for the future. But don't worry to the point that it ruins your present life. Don't worry about the color of your hair, how big your feet may be right now or if you have curly hair. Jesus says that what counts is whether or not you have your spiritual act together. That means making sure you are a Christian and that you are seeking to develop your spiritual life as well as your mental, social or physical life. Keep your priorities straight!

FIFTH DAY
THEME: A LIFE WORTH LIVING
Read Mark 5:1-20

In the course of His travels, Jesus met a lot of peculiar individuals. I don't think any were as unusual as the man from Gerasene. (Read the passage.)

Wow, what a weird individual! Can you imagine having someone like that living in your neighborhood? This man really had some problems. He lived a pretty miserable life and he had no purpose at all—until he met Jesus.

Look at the change that took place in his life after he began a relationship with Jesus! He was changed in two areas. (Read v. 15.) This man was clothed (an outward change) and his right mind restored (an inward change). Once you have become a Christian there will probably be some noticeable changes in your life too. Most people see change pretty soon after a decision is made.

The best part of all is that Jesus gave this man a new purpose in life. He gave him a ministry or job to do. (Read vv. 19-20.) This man was given the assignment of telling his friends about Jesus. Why do you think his friends would believe him? (Let them respond.) That's right, because they saw the difference that a relationship with Jesus had made in his life.

What changes has He made in your life? Does your life have purpose and direction? Have you told anyone about the Lord since you became a Christian? Have you told anyone lately? Would they believe you if you did? Why?

SIXTH DAY
THEME: MAKING IT LAST
Read John 15:1-11

It seems as if nothing lasts for very long these days. The car we buy today will be broken in no time at all. The radio or television we purchase today will only last a few short years. Does anything really last?

Perhaps you may be wondering tonight whether or not the decision you made at camp this week will last very long after you get home. There are some things you can do to be sure that it does last. Let me read a passage of Scripture to you that should help. (Read John 15:1-11.)

The Bible says that if we want our walk with the Lord to continue for many years, we need to be sure we stay close to Him. We do that by reading the Bible and spending time in prayer each day. That is how we "abide." The word abide really just means to stay close. It is natural for us to drift away from God so be sure you stop yourself as soon as you detect it. Ask Him to forgive you when you make mistakes and never quit reading the Bible or praying.

Picture your life like that of a branch of grapes. As soon as the branch leaves the vine it begins to die. The fruit dries up and withers. As Christians we need to stay attached to our source of nourishment—the Bible. Determine how you will spend at least a few minutes of each day reading the Bible and praying when you get home. That is how you will stay healthy and make your commitment last for a long, long time.

Cabin Devotionals
for
Senior High Campers

FIRST DAY
THEME: THE GREATER NEED
Read Mark 2:1-12

Many of you have come to camp to have a good time. I have no doubt that you will too. But I think all of us have also come because we have certain needs. Maybe you have a need to make some more friends, or to take a vacation from work or school. Perhaps you are like the man in the story. He had a need too. His need was to be made healthy. Jesus saw this man and realized that although he needed better health, what he needed more was to be forgiven of his sins.

Perhaps God is looking at you tonight in the same way that He was looking at this man. He sees your particular need but realizes you have a far greater need which you may not even know about. As in the case with this man, God desires to provide for your spiritual needs as well as for your social or emotional needs. I hope you take the time to allow God to meet your needs this week in the spiritual dimension of your life as well.

SECOND DAY
THEME: THE BALANCED LIFE
Read Luke 2:41-52

Not a lot is known about the life of Jesus during His high school years. But there is a story that tells us what He was like as He was entering His teen years. Let me read it to you. (Read the passage.)

Apparently Jesus faced a lot of the same problems you face. There were times when He was misunderstood by His family, times when He wanted to be alone, times when He just had other things to do with His time than what others wanted. We forget the fact that although Jesus was the Son of God, He was also a boy at one time too. Pay particular attention to what He was like then.

(Read v. 52 again.) This verse tells us that His greatest priorities revolved around four basic areas: the mental (wisdom), physical (stature), spiritual (favor with God) and the social (favor with man). Jesus lived a balanced life as a teenager. Many of you are concerned about sports, being liked at school by your friends, doing well at school, etc. But do you consider your spiritual needs too? Jesus realized that unless He had that dimension of His life together, the other three areas were of little benefit to Him. Is your life balanced today? What are the areas that put your life out of balance? What should you do about it? Like a tire on a car, if your life is not in balance it will not be as effective.

THIRD DAY
THEME: THE ULTIMATE SINNER?
Read John 8:2-11

Our society places a lot of emphasis upon certain sins. It was that way in Jesus' day too. They seemed to think that adultery was one of the ultimate sins in life. They didn't realize that all sin is wrong in God's eyes. Let me read this story to show you what I mean. (Read the passage.)

These men who brought the woman in to see Jesus were every bit as guilty of sin as this woman. But look, even though this woman had committed a sin that was bad, Jesus still forgave her. Maybe none of us have ever committed a sin like the one committed by this woman but we have all done something wrong. God says in James 2:10-11 that if we break one law of His we are guilty of breaking them all. Every one of us falls into that category.

But the good news is this: just as Jesus desired to forgive this woman, He desires to forgive us too. No matter what sins we have committed in life Jesus can and wants to forgive us. All we have to do is ask Him. Maybe now is the time you need to do that as we lie here in our bunks. (Close in a time of prayer. Perhaps lead them in a sample prayer that they can pray to themselves.)

FOURTH DAY
THEME: A PURPOSE IN EVERY PROBLEM
Read Matthew 14:22-33

A lot of people have problems these days and our society is no different than any other in that respect. Man has always had times when he didn't understand what was happening to him. Have you ever had experiences like that? (Let them respond.) What are some of the problems that average teenagers face today? (Let the discussion run for a few minutes.)

Peter went through a pretty big problem in his life one day. I'm sure he was probably asking himself, "Why me God?" Let's read it together. (Read the passage.)

God doesn't always cause the problems that come into our lives but He does allow them to occur and He knows which ones we have. Oftentimes there is a lesson that we should learn that will help us in life. What was the lesson that Jesus wanted to teach Peter in this situation? (Did he need to trust God for help?) Peter learned the important lesson of applied faith. It may be a lesson we need to learn too. Jesus cared about Peter enough to allow this problem to come into his life. He knew that Peter needed to learn this lesson and that he would be a better person because of it.

What are some of the problems that you face now and how can God be trying to teach you lessons? What kinds of lessons might He be teaching you? Can you see that your problems are not there because God has left you? He is only one arm's length away—even in the midst of the storm!

FIFTH DAY
THEME: SOME THINGS TAKE TIME
Read Luke 9:57-62 and Matthew 19:27-30

We live in a world that wants everything done as fast as possible. We eat fast food, have instant printing and laundry and our photographs are developed within an hour, etc. We hate to wait! But why? Some things just take time in life, however, and maturing in your walk with the Lord is one of them.

A man came to Jesus one day who thought he could pay the price of becoming a Christian. He found out he couldn't. The disciples were already deciding who would get what in the new kingdom. They weren't wasting any time about it! Ever feel like that too?

Living the Christian life isn't easy. There are no instant Christians either. It takes a lot of hard work, tenacity and discipline. Don't get caught up thinking there is a short cut. There isn't! If you really want to grow as a Christian you'll have to do what everyone else does. You'll need to read the Bible on a daily basis. You'll also need to spend time in prayer each day. Memorize passages of Scripture and take the time to help people in need.

The word disciple and discipline come from the same root word. There's a reason for that. Some things just take time in life and growing as a Christian is one of them. Don't get discouraged if you don't see progress. Sometimes you won't see it until after a period of time has passed. Keep at it!

SIXTH DAY
THEME: QUALITIES THAT COUNT
Read Galatians 5:16-24

Many high school teenagers think that if they can just drive the fastest car, date the cutest guy or girl on campus or wear the right clothes, etc., *then* they'll be a real success in life. What kinds of things do you or your friends associate with success? (Let them respond.)

God has a different measuring stick than that however. He gives us His qualities in the book of Galatians. He tells us the qualities of a person who is missing out in life and the qualities of one who is a real success. (Read the passage.) Which ones do you possess?

The qualities of love, joy, peace, etc. are all qualities that you cannot buy with money although a lot of money *is* spent in their pursuit. God says you can have them by following Him. As we live our life the way God designed it to be lived we become recipients of these qualities. I hope each of you desire these in life.

As you go through your last few years of high school you'll see a lot of people trying to get these qualities. Remember, they're yours for the taking as you commit your life to God on a daily basis.

Notes

Chapter 1

1. Reprinted from "Guiding Principles for Christian Camping," National Sunday School Association, Wheaton, Illinois.

Chapter 2

1. C. E. Hendry, "A Cooperative Study of Counselors," *Association Boys' Work Journal* (May, 1931), p. 44.
2. Mitchell and Crawford, *Camp Counseling* (Philadelphia: W.B. Saunders Co., 1961), pp. 40-44.

Chapter 5

1. Mitchell and Crawford, *Camp Counseling* (Philadelphia: W.B. Saunders Co., 1961), pp. 84-86.

Chapter 6

1. Elmer Ott, *So You Want to Be a Camp Counselor* (New York: Association Press, 1946), pp. 29-32.

Chapter 7

1. Rudolf Dreikurs, *Children: The Challenge* (Duell, Sloan and Pearce, 1964).
2. Adapted from material submitted to Mrs. Papworth by Dr. Woolitz, Principal, Loma Portal Elementary School. Distributed by Adult Education Department, San Diego Schools.

Chapter 8

1. G. Keith Olson, *Counseling Teenagers* (Loveland, CO: Group Books, 1984), p. 57.

Bibliography

Books

Bairstow, Jeffrey. *Four Season Camping*. New York: Random House, Inc., 1982.

Bast, Rochelle, ed. *Handbook for Senior Adult Camping*. Eugene, OR: University of Oregon, 1977.

Beck, Helen L. *Going to Camp*. New York: Stephen Dave Press, 1950.

A Bibliography of Camp Safety, Hygiene and Sanitation. New York: National Safety Council.

Bonnell, John. *Psychology for Pastor and People*. New York: Harper & Row Pubs., Inc., 1960.

Camp Commission. *Guiding Principles for Christian Camping*. Chicago: National Sunday School Association, 1962.

Carra, Andrew J., ed., *Camping*. Briarcliff Manor, NY: Stein & Day, 1978.

Church Camping for Junior Highs. Philadelphia: The Westminster Press.

Corbin, H. Dan. *Recreation Leadership*. Englewood Cliffs: Prentice-Hall, Inc., 1953.

Cunningham, Ruth. *Understanding Group Behavior of Boys and Girls*. Teachers College, Columbia University.

Des Grey, Arthur H. *Camping*. The Ronald Press Co., 1950.

Dimock, Hedley S. *Administration of the Modern Camp*. New York: Association Press, 1948.

Dobbins, Gaines S. *Winning the Children*. Nashville: Broadman Press, 1953.

Doty, Richard S. *The Character Dimension of Camping*. New York: Association Press, 1960.

Dreikurs, Rudolf, and Soltz, Vicki. *Children: The Challenge*. New York: E. P. Dutton, 1964.

———. *Psychology in the Classroom*. New York: Harper & Row Pubs., Inc., 1968.

Driver, Helen, and Contributors. *Counseling and Learning Through Small Group Discussions*. Wisconsin: Monona Publications, 1958.

Ensign, John and Ruth. *Camping Together as Christians*. Atlanta, GA: John Knox Press.

Good Counselors Make Good Camps. #19-530, Girl Scouts.

Goodrich, Lois. *Decentralized Camping*. Martinsville, IN: American Camping Assn., 1982.

Guiding Principles for Christian Camping. National Sunday School Association, 1962.

Hartwig, Marie, and Myers, Bettye. *Children Are Human (Even at Camp), and Children Are Human (If the Counselors Really Know Them)*. Minneapolis: Burgess Publishing Co., 1961, 1962.

Hartwig, Marie. *Workbook for Camp Counselor Training*. Minneapolis:

Burgess Publishing Co.,1960.

Hurlock, Elizabeth B. *Adolescent Development.* New York: McGraw-Hill Co., 1973.

Joy, Barbara Ellen. *Annotated Bibliography on Camping.* Chicago: American Camping Association, 1950.

_____. *Camp Craft.* Minneapoilis: Burgess Publishing Co., 1955.

_____. *Camping.* Minneapolis: Burgess Publishing Co., 1957.

_____. *Cooperative Committee Plan in Camps.* Camp Publications.

_____. *Professional Relationships in Camp.* Camp Publications, #6.

_____. *Suggestions for Responsibilities of Counselors for Care of Campers.* Camp Publications, #9.

Kesting, Ted. *The Outdoor Encyclopedia.* San Diego: A. S. Barnes and Co., Inc., 1957.

Klein, Alan, and Irwin Haladner. *It's Wise to Supervise.* Toronto: Canadian Camping Association.

Knowles, Malcolm S., and Hilda F. *How to Develop Better Leaders.* New York: Association Press, 1955.

Kraus, Richard, and Scanlin, Margery. *Introduction to Camp Counseling.* Englewood Cliffs, NJ: Prentice-Hall, Inc., 1983.

Laird, Donald A., and Laird, Eleanor C. *The New Psychology for Leadership.* Westport, CT: Green Wood Press, 1975.

Ledlie, John A., and Holbein, Francis W. *Camp Counselor's Manual.* rev. ed. New York: Association Press, 1969.

Lindgren, Henry Clay. *Effective Leadership in Human Relations.*

Lindholm, Major Mauno A. *Camping and Outdoor Fun.* New York: Hart Publishing Co., 1959.

Lynn, Gordon. *Camping and Camp Crafts.* New York: Golden Books, 1959.

Mackay, Joy. *Creative Camping.* rev. ed. Wheaton, IL: Victor Books, 1984.

_____. *Raindrops Keep Falling on My Tent.* Martinsville, IN: American Camping Assn., 1981.

MacInnes, Gordon A. *A Guide to Worship in Camp and Conference.* Philadelphia: The Westminster Press.

Mangan, Doreen, and Fehr, Terry. *How to Be a Super Camp Counselor.* New York: Watts, Franklin, Inc., 1979.

Mattson, Lloyd D. *Camping Guideposts: Christian Camp Counselor's Handbook.* Chicago: Moody Press, 1962.

Menninger, William C. *How to Be a Successful Teen-ager.* New York: Sterling Publishing Co., Inc., 1954.

Mitchell, A. Viola, and Meier, Joel F. *Camp Counseling.* 6th ed. Philadelphia: Saunders College Publishing, 1983.

Mitchell, Grace. *Fundamentals of Day Camping.* Martinsville, IN: American Camping Assn., 1982.

Peterson, Doris T. *Your Family Goes Camping*. Nashville: Abingdon Press, 1959.

Raymer, Mrs. Ralph H. *The Counselors' Job at Camp*. Ontario Camping Assn.

Roscoe, D.T. *Your Book of Camping*. Winchester, MA: Faber & Faber, Inc., 1980.

Stutts, Evelyn C. *All That You Need to Know About Camp Counseling*. Newport Beach, CA: Charlton House Publishing, 1981.

Todd, Floyd and Pauline. *Camping for Christian Youth*. New York: Harper and Row, 1963.

Presbyterian Church (U.S.A.) *The Young Adolescent in the Church*. Board of Christian Education.

Webb, Kenneth B., ed. *Light from a Thousand Campfires*. New York: Association Press, 1960.

Wentzel, Fred D., and Schlingman, Edward L. *The Counselor's Job*. New York: Association Press.

Magazine Articles

Anthony, Michael. "Training: Key to Quality Staff and Programs." *Journal of Christian Camping*, May-June, 1985, p. 6.

Ashmen, John and Mattocks, Ron. "Preparing for Crisis Situations." *Journal of Christian Camping*, July-August, 1985.

Crook, Donald C. "Training Equals Counselor Effectiveness." *Journal of Christian Camping*, May-June, 1982.

Drahn, Gloria. "The Call to Camping Is Addictive." *Journal of Christian Camping*, September-October, 1985, p. 24.

Drovdahl, Robert. "Communication Key to Counseling." *Journal of Christian Camping*, May-June, 1982.

Fawver, Gary. "Taking the Church Outdoors." *Journal of Christian Camping*, November-December, 1982.

Hansell, Tim. "Holy Sweat." *Journal of Christian Camping*, May-June, 1982.

Healy, Edward. "Leadership—Some Aims for the Future." *Camping Magazine*, American Camping Association, February, 1956.

Henderson, Eva Lee. "Age Group Characteristics: Key to Understanding Kids." *Journal of Christian Camping*, March-April, 1984.

Josselyn, Dr. Irene. "Psychological Needs of the Overprivileged Child." *Camping Magazine*, American Camping Association, June, 1952.

Leonard, A. T., and VanHartesvedlt, Fred. "How Understanding Child Behavior Can Improve Counselor-Camper Relationships." *Camping Magazine*, American Camping Association, January, 1957.

Mattson, Lloyd. "Bible Study Helps Counselors Minister." *Journal of Christian Camping*, July-August, 1983.

_____. "Camping and the Church." *Journal of Christian Camping*, May-June, 1984.

Pioneer MInistries. "Age Group Characteristics." *Journal of Christian Camping*, March-April, 1984.

Schmotzer, James. "Child Abuse: What Can We Do?" *Journal of Christian Camping*, January-February, 1985, p. 6.

Short, Allison. "Bible Curriculum Options for Camp. " *Journal of Christian Camping*, May-June, 1983.

_____. "Choosing Bible Study Materials for Your Camp." *Journal of Christian Camping*, January-February, 1985, p. 14.

_____. "Values Education at Camp." *Journal of Christian Camping*, July-August, 1982.

Staires, Sally. "Counselor Job Description." *Journal of Christian Camping*, July-August, 1985, p. 21.

White, Stan. "The Counselor's Role in Camper Discipline." *Journal of Christian Camping*, January-February, 1982.

Films

Axemanship. Peter McLarin demonstrates the use and care of various types of axes. How to chop down a tree, split logs, and cut firewood. 9 min., sd., b&w. Boy Scouts.

Boats, Motors and People. Emphasis on safety. 30 min., sd., b&w or color. American Red Cross.

Camp Time, Any Time! Camping including nature mobile, rock collecting, clearing a stream, weather station, clay firing, canoeing, waterfront, trail signs, primitive unit, songs, etc. 22 min., sd., color. Girl Scouts.

Camping Education. The program at National Camp for training professional camp leaders. 2 reels, sd., b&w, (college & adult). LIFE.

Canoe Country. The Watsons take a canoe trip along an old fur route. Fishing, swimming, and setting up camp. Keeping matches dry, how to use campfires safely, and how to carry a canoe. 15 min., sd., color (elementary-college). National Film Board of Canada.

Help Wanted. Basic principles of first aid and caring for victims before the doctor arrives. Prepared under the supervision of prominent physicians and surgeons. 22 min. U.S. Public Health Service.

Overnight. Group and leader plan and enjoy overnight camping trip. All participate in group planning. 2 reels, color or b&w, (junior high—college). Girl Scouts.

Wilderness Day. Canoe and camping trip on the lakes of Northern Minnesota with preparation of shelters, handling fires, cooking, waste disposal, proper canoe handling, 29 min., color. U of Minn.

Youth in Camps. Decentralized, "Camptivity" plan of camping. 2 reels, sd., (college). Life.

Index